South Africa's
Security Dilemmas

THE WASHINGTON PAPERS

. . . intended to meet the need for an authoritative, yet prompt, public appraisal of the major developments in world affairs.

Series Editors: Walter Laqueur; Amos A. Jordan

Associate Editors: William J. Taylor, Jr.; Thomas Bleha

Executive Editor: Jean C. Newsom

Managing Editor: Nancy B. Eddy

President, CSIS: Amos A. Jordan

MANUSCRIPT SUBMISSION

The Washington Papers and Praeger Publishers welcome inquiries concerning manuscript submissions. Please include with your inquiry a curriculum vitae, synopsis, table of contents, and estimated manuscript length. Manuscripts must be between 120–200 double-spaced typed pages. All submissions will be peer reviewed. Submissions to *The Washington Papers* should be sent to *The Washington Papers*; The Center for Strategic and International Studies; 1800 K Street NW; Suite 400; Washington, DC 20006. Book proposals should be sent to Praeger Publishers; One Madison Avenue; New York NY 10010.

South Africa's Security Dilemmas

Christopher Coker

Foreword by Kenneth W. Grundy

Published with The Center for
Strategic and International Studies
Washington, D.C.

PRAEGER

New York
Westport, Connecticut
London

Library of Congress Cataloging-in-Publication Data

Coker, Christopher.
  South Africa's security dilemmas.

  (The Washington papers; ISSN 0278-937X, vol. XIV, 126)
  "Published with the Center for Strategic and
International Studies,
Washington, D.C."
   1. South Africa – National security.   I. Title.
II. Series.
UA856.C57   1987   355'.033068   87-2437
ISBN 0-275-92771-7 (alk. paper)
ISBN 0-275-92772-5 (pbk.)

The *Washington Papers* are written under the auspices of The Center
for Strategic and International Studies (CSIS) and published
with CSIS by Praeger Publishers. The views expressed in these papers are
those of the authors and not necessarily those of The Center.

Library of Congress Catalog Card Number: 87-2437
ISBN: 0-275-92771-7 (cloth)
       0-275-92772-5 (paper)

First published in 1987

Praeger Publishers, One Madison Avenue, New York, NY 10010
A division of Greenwood Press, Inc.

Printed in the United States of America

∞

The paper used in this book complies with the Permanent
Paper Standard issued by the National Information Standards
Organization (Z39.48-1984).

10 9 8 7 6 5 4 3 2 1

Contents

Foreword

Since it became clear that the white minority regime in South Africa would not fall of its own weight, political analysts have looked more seriously and systematically at Pretoria's arms of state. Numerous studies of South Africa's diverse armed formations and of its strategic planning and security problems, both foreign and domestic, have been published in recent years. The study of South Africa's security has gone from a virtually underdeveloped scholarly enterprise at the start of the 1980s, to a growth industry.

The first reports sought to provide an inventory of formations and force levels and to explore the balance of forces in the southern African cockpit. But much of that research is descriptive, derivative, and repetitive. As interest grew, and as more scholars staked out their claims, Pretoria sought to deny them access to reliable data. The very same insecurity and secretiveness that prompt the constraints on the media regarding civil unrest close doors on the most sensitive data of all, the strategic and security dimensions of state policy.

There was a time when public documents were a gold mine of information, especially if approached selectively and critically. Some regard parliament as the only quasi-objective source of information under the state of emergency. Yet, even in parliament, government discloses less and less under the generalized excuse that disclosure would not be in South Africa's interests. The press too is muffled on security issues.

The sorts of data that I compiled back in the late 1970s and early 1980s would not be made public today. A kind of inflation exists about defense studies, as more and more scholars chase after less and less data. Consequently, a premium is placed on balance, skepticism, judgment, and criticism. I think Christopher Coker's work stands solidly as mature scholarship. He wends his way carefully through these data deficiencies and he provides sober and critical analysis.

There is much that I disagree with in his study, particularly with regard to interpretation and emphasis. For example, I do not share Coker's views about the political neutrality of the military, about militarization (which I see as a process), or about South Africa's commitment to the Nkomati accord. But that is the way it is with important and controversial questions. And that is the strength of this monograph — it asks the right questions, and it tries to answer them seriously and thoughtfully. Coker challenges many of the common assumptions about South Africa's security establishment.

For example, Coker doubts, correctly I think, whether the policymakers in Pretoria really do have a single viable defense strategy. He asks if their military options are more limited than we imagine. He critiques the proposition that the South African Defense Force is a colossus among dwarves. He reasons that for a state confronted by a variety of immediate security problems, defense budgets are relatively small, procurement is casual, force levels are minimal, and commitment by the white population is suspect.

Too often commentators perceive of capability analysis as a kind of mechanistic balance sheet, with pluses and minuses that can be measured and quantified. Most studies about South African security seem to be based on that assumption. They focus on the tangible factors of power —

numbers of troops, inventories of materiel, GNP, and so forth. And they often conclude that, barring interference from outside the region, South Africa is invincible. But the reductionist perspective neglects the intangibles – morale, commitment, leadership, purpose. And it tends to overlook the domestic sociopolitical dimensions. Coker questions the efficacy of this kind of thinking.

Coker also raises the time variable, seldom discussed in the literature. He demonstrates how sanctions might take a serious toll on South African defense. Weaponry and equipment can be expended in combat, and they can become obsolescent. Replacements may be long in planning, slow in coming, and costly. The regime's constituents may resist committing extensive financial resources for unclear ends.

The challenge to Pretoria will not be solved simply by throwing more troops or greater fire power into the contest, even if they were politically feasible options. The struggle for South Africa is at heart a political dispute rather than a military one.

Christopher Coker's fine monograph gets you thinking in useful directions. His study is not the final word, there may never be "the" final word, but it sharpens and and focuses your thinking. That is its strength and its purpose.

Kenneth W. Grundy
Professor of Political Science
Case Western Reserve University

About the Author

Christopher Coker is Lecturer in International Relations at the London School of Economics. He is the author of *The United States and South Africa 1968–86: Constructive Engagement and its Critics* (Duke University Press, 1986) and *NATO, the Warsaw Pact and Africa* (Macmillan, 1985). He has also written an earlier *Washington Paper* (no. 111), on *The Soviet Union, Eastern Europe, and the New International Economic Order* (1984). He is a frequent contributor to such journals as *African Affairs, The Journal of Modern African Studies, International Affairs, Politique Etrangère, Europa-Archiv,* and *Survival.*

Acknowledgments

I would like to thank the Nuffield Foundation for a generous grant that made possible a visit to South Africa in the spring and summer of 1986. I would also like to acknowledge the assistance of Simon Baynham, John Seiler, Jack Spence, and Stanley Uys, as well as many people in South Africa who provided invaluable advice, yet would prefer to remain anonymous.

1

The South African Defense Force: Myth and Reality

> "Army": a class of non-producers who defend the nation by devouring everything likely to tempt an enemy to invade.
> — Ambrose Bierce, *The Enlarged Devil's Dictionary*

In September 1984, immediately prior to the political disturbances that were about to engulf the Eastern Cape, the South African Defense Force (SADF) mounted the largest military exercise since World War II. Watched by President P. W. Botha and his entire cabinet, the operation was an impressive, even daunting display of military strength.

To the outside world South Africa has always appeared to be a military power of the first rank, possibly the only state in Africa that can claim to be so. The post-Sharpeville years witnessed a massive expansion of the SADF, which had grown hardly at all after World War II.

The Permanent Force rose by 65 percent, the Citizen Force sixfold. Before 1960 the armed services had accounted for less than 1 percent of the country's gross national product (GNP) and less than 7 percent of the government budget. Between 1960–1965, defense spending rose to 3 percent of GNP and 21 percent of the budget (not including outlays for the police), and by the end of the decade 30 percent in all. The increase in South Africa's military strength corresponded neither to the external environment in which the Republic found itself nor to the internal pressures faced by the regime. It represented what can only be described as a form of overinsurance, a quest for security, an affirmation of political power in a world in which the Republic found itself isolated and shunned.

If the rate of expansion leveled off briefly at the end of the decade it did so only to rise again between 1974-1977. Manpower grew as the terms of national service were extended from 12 months to 24. At the same time, mindful of the arms embargo, the South Africans built up the tenth largest arms industry in the world. The state-run Arms Corporation of South Africa (ARMSCOR) grew 30 times, its annual rate of procurement exceeding one billion rands (R) between 1968-1978. An increased emphasis was placed on local assembly and local content even of armaments produced under license to Italian and French companies. By the late 1970s South Africa was able to manufacture most of its weapons from modern fighters to locally produced tanks. The arms embargo appeared to have little, if any, impact, except in the higher reaches of technology.

In the light of this recent history it was not altogether surprising that the world believed South Africa to be militarily strong and growing stronger. As early as 1970 one authority had already concluded that direct military intervention against the Republic would be impossible without the generous backing of a superpower.[1] In October 1977 the *Washington Post* felt constrained to observe: "Compared to any of the black African countries on or near its borders South Africa has a huge arsenal and a military expertise that is far superior to any of them now or in the near future." As the years passed the strength of the SADF became a compelling political reality that was difficult to ignore or dismiss. If societies, like stones, crack along their lines of weakness, the armed forces seemed to represent one of the state's major strengths.

Given that defense spending in 1977, a year after the

Soweto uprising, accounted for a third of all military expenditure in Africa (excluding Egypt) and that the SADF's mobilizable strength on paper was 400,000—larger than that of any other sub-Saharan state—it seemed reasonable to conclude that "by almost any conventional index of national military power, the Republic of South Africa continues to tower over any current or foreseeable African opponent or coalition."[2] This view prevailed even after the influx of Soviet arms and Cuban troops in the region during the Angolan civil war (1975–1976). At the end of the 1970s the authors of a book provocatively entitled *Why South Africa Will Survive* contended that because it was the only sub-Saharan African state with an industrial and logistic infrastructure strong enough to maintain unaided a reasonably up-to-date system of land, air, and sea defense, no African state, even with Soviet assistance, would "pose even a potential threat to the South Africans for years and probably decades" to come.[3] If anything, South Africa's recent incursions into neighboring countries have served to reinforce this conclusion despite the violence that has broken out in South Africa itself.

Quite apart from its accuracy, there is every reason why this picture should not go unchallenged. In this paper I wish to call into question some common assumptions that are either untrue or of doubtful validity. I wish to ask in particular whether South Africa has a viable defense strategy or whether its military options are more limited than we imagine; whether its military power is not already under threat from low defense spending and declining service morale; and whether the Republic is quite as formidable a power as it is frequently portrayed. Indeed, as the South African state begins to founder we might ask three pertinent questions about the real picture:

• Can South Africans discharge basic tasks: defending the border against high or low-intensity threats and maintaining internal security? Each involves a number of subtasks. On the basis of Frederick the Great's maxim that

attack is the best form of defense, operations beyond the
frontier require air supremacy, a long-range air-to-ground
delivery ordnance capability, and ground-combat projection
and sustainability. Countering civil disorder in the townships demands different requirements still: response command and control, appropriate weapons and training, and,
if the present violence spills over into the countryside as it
may well do over the next few years, the capability to conduct small-scale surgical operations. Over time, the basic
elements of the SADF do not, on the whole, appear well
suited to either mission. Air and ground units are currently
adequate for the "pro-active" mission — taking the war to
South Africa's neighbors — but obsolescence will soon erode
these capabilities without substantial outside assistance.
The South African Air Force (SAAF) is increasingly threatened by the most extensive ground-to-air missile system
the Soviet Union has ever installed outside Syria and the
Warsaw Pact. At home, equipment, organization, manning,
and morale appear to be major deficiencies. The small number of attack helicopters in the army's inventory could pose
a major problem in rural contingencies, although not as
crippling as inadequate training and low troop morale. Because these problems are likely to mount it seems worth
examining each at length.

• A second question is whether South Africa has de-
rived much political return from the use of military force.
The raids into Botswana, Zimbabwe, and Zambia that sabotaged the Commonwealth mission in June 1986 and the
recent use of troops to quell township unrest have reinforced the picture of a massive state security apparatus, an
impression that even at home has lulled the government
into thinking that it can fall back upon force as an instrument of last resort. In fact, South Africans seem to be
complacently living in the past. There is a real risk that
they could find themselves in a serious military predica-
ment by the early 1990s as the state comes under increasing pressure from civil unrest at home and escalating violence on the frontier. It may be convenient, of course, to go

on pretending otherwise, to continue imagining that South Africa enjoys a relative margin of strength – indeed, a degree of regional influence it would not enjoy *but* for the successful application of military power. In reality, however, South Africa's military strength has been eroding for some years. To date there is no sign that the government or the military have focused on whether the state can begin the long process of reversing that decline or whether it would even be desirable given the speed of political change in the Republic itself. It will probably accelerate still further if only because it mirrors the domestic crisis within the country: a reluctance to face the truth of the regime's position and to learn from its past mistakes.

• A final reason for questioning many of the analyses of the 1970s is provided by some of the seminal changes that have taken place in South Africa itself: the decision to maintain a ceiling on military spending in the hope of further reducing a disproportionately large budget deficit; the growing stress of national service in an army that relies so heavily on conscription; and an escalating crisis in the arms industry that has produced low stockpiles and even lower rates of production.

These internal factors rarely received much discussion in pamphlets and books that were published 10 years ago, many of which tended to treat the country's military establishment as one of the few enduring landmarks in an otherwise uncertain political landscape. Collectively, however, all three questions have begun to raise serious doubts about the reality of the "garrison state" and the willingness of the regime to retreat into a hypothetical *laager*, a term referring to the defensive formation of wagons the Boers used during the Great Trek into the interior. South Africa, it would seem, can either go forward or back but, unlike the Red Queen in *Through the Looking Glass*, cannot continue to mark time.

It is worth adding one final rider. In discussing the SADF's weaknesses and focusing so little on its strengths,

one must be careful not to detract from its innate profes-
sionalism. Relative to other African armies, the SADF's
strengths are not a political fiction. At present the SADF
has a quantitative advantage in functioning equipment in
the possible war zones and a qualitative advantage in conventional weapons and maintenance. In addition, the training and motivation of its troops is still vastly superior. On
the other hand, the evidence that these elements are beginning to represent diminishing assets – in some cases
promissory notes that can never be cashed – is continually
mounting. The warning signs are already manifest for anyone who cares to look for them. In the case of South Africa,
one should always take account of Ralph Hodgson's timely
warning that "the handwriting on the wall may well be a
forgery." Nevertheless, the West will have only itself to
blame for not deciphering its meaning in time.

2

The Enemy Within

Why this sudden bewilderment, this confusion?
(How serious people's faces have become)
Why are the streets and squares emptying so rapidly
Everyone going home lost in thought?

Because night has fallen and the barbarians haven't
    come
And some of our men just in from the border say
There are no barbarians any longer.

Now what's going to happen to us without barbarians?
They were, those people, a kind of solution.

> — C. P. Cavafy, "Waiting for the Barbarians"

Although the SADF has been trained to fight a traditional counterinsurgency war since the Pondoland revolt in the early 1960s, the prospect of such a conflict is nevertheless rather remote. The border with Mozambique with its military bases and extensive network of roads, electric fences, and mined shrubland cleared to a depth of a mile might seem to confirm the opinion of the former head of the SADF's general operations that South Africa has already entered a stage of classical insurgency.[4] For the military, the

African National Congress (ANC) may still be a potent
force – revolutionaries in search of a revolution, dedicated to
what the writer Jacques Ellul has called *le terrorisme sim-
plificateur*.[5] The movement's operational record, however, is
not striking.

The army is not sanguine about the sabotage of such
prestige targets as nuclear power stations or even "soft targets" – government or military personnel – but for the most
part such attacks are infrequent or exaggerated by the
press. Quite apart from the fact that South Africa itself
sponsors a two-way traffic in terrorism – training Mozambique National Resistance (MNR) guerrillas in the years
before the Nkomati accord and Bishop Abel Muzorewa's
auxiliaries in camps in the northern Transvaal, even allowing Ntsu Makhehle's Lesotho Liberation Army (LLA) un-
impeded transit through the Orange Free State – the ANC
has never put much stress on the classic guerrilla struggle
largely because the conditions are so unfavorable in the
circumstances that it confronts. The ANC's potential to
conduct a guerrilla war is limited; its main training bases
and supply dumps are far away; its infiltration routes into
South Africa are long and insecure. Its leaders are the first
to acknowledge that there exists a tremendous logistical
problem for armed struggle. Although industrial sabotage
and attacks on "soft targets" will doubtless continue, it was
made clear at an ANC conference in the summer of 1985
that the movement attached far more importance to popular armed force and insurrection – "actively drawing the
masses into the prosecution of a people's war." (Message of
the ANC National Executive, August 8, 1985).

Yet even today the power of the state is all-pervasive. As
the American scholar Diana Russell noted 20 years ago,
attempting to account for the fact that a revolution in
South Africa still seemed far off when the conditions
seemed so propitious, it was not the "push for rebellion
which is weak but the obstacles [which] are so enormous".[6]
Nothing has really changed. The movement of the population is still controlled; townships can be sealed off from the

rest of the country whenever they explode into revolt; the countryside may be vast but it is sparsely populated, except for the homelands. And they can be cordoned off, if to judge from recent attacks on the capital, Umtata, some — like Transkei — may be providing new infiltration routes for the ANC.

Although the pass law system has now been scrapped, the population can still be "corralled," directed to "suitable areas" for employment — a codeword for "controlled urbanization." In recent months the government has built a whole series of new townships such as Soshanguve and Bothshabelo, well away from existing white metropolitan areas, in keeping with its program of "group related settlements." In the future, the authorities may be able to contain outbreaks of violence even more effectively than at present.[7]

Nor should we forget that the total number of guerrilla incidents in the first nine months of 1985 was only 93, only 37 more than the whole of 1983, the previous record year.[8] The number is hardly significant considering that the townships were in flames. Indeed, a breakdown of the figures of armed incidents during this period compared with the figures of damage to property in civil disturbances is especially instructive. Two railway lines, eight government and public buildings, six power installations, one fuel depot, seventeen businesses, three military buildings, three houses, three police stations, and three waterpipelines were destroyed in guerrilla attacks. Forty-eight civilians and policemen were also attacked or killed in incidents, not all of which were directly attributable to the ANC. Compared with this toll, confrontations between rioting groups and the security forces that ended in serious injury or loss of life took place in more than 100 urban and rural townships in 1985. In April alone there were 1,549 incidents in all. Between September 1984 and July 1986 a total of 985 businesses, 1,272 schools, 3,902 private homes, 937 homes of policemen, 8,773 delivery vehicles, and 6,815 buses were seriously damaged or destroyed in incidents of political unrest.[9]

In short, the violent disorder in the townships presented the government with a far more serious challenge than
the threat of insurgency. Unlike previous outbreaks of violence it was sustained for months on end and appeared to be
endemic, not cyclical. True, fewer than 20 whites lost their
lives, but the deaths of more than 1,200 blacks—more than
double the total in the Soweto uprising—did more than the
ANC could have hoped to discredit the regime in the eyes of
the international community, to undermine white morale
and the support of the government by the business community, to erode—in a word—some of the very obstacles to
revolution and revolt to which Russell had drawn attention
20 years earlier.

Policing the Townships

The township riots remain by far the most serious challenge
the security forces now face, not in their immediate impact
but on their long-term implications. For they are above all
a major threat to the policy of coopting black leaders
and creating black institutions at the local level, a prospect
that remains the government's only hope of defusing social
tension, its only real prospect of what the Germans call
Verlegenheitslosung—finding a way out of an impossible
situation.

    The armed forces have always been unqualified in their
support of the reform program, never concealing the fact
that they would be hard-pressed to deal with a revolution
were one to break out. As General Boshoff warned in 1977,
before the first reforms were implemented,

> the anti-revolutionary struggle is 80% socio-economic
> and 20% military. If South Africa lost the socio-eco-
> nomic struggle we need not bother to fight the military
> one. The objective is no longer territory, but the hearts
> and minds of men.[10]

Or to quote General Constand Viljoen writing in 1981, "a basic principle in the revolutionary struggle is to remove the sting of the revolution by making early changes . . . from a position of strength," a principle, which from a strictly "security point of view," he held to be "among the highest priorities."[11]

In passing, it is interesting to note that Boshoff's statement conveys an unconscious echo of Joseph Stalin's celebrated remark to Milovan Djilas that armies in the modern era no longer occupy territory for its own sake but to establish a new socioeconomic order in place of the old. In the case of South Africa, however, the army has found itself underpowered to police, let alone enforce, the new socioeconomic dispensation that the government had tried to introduce by transfering limited powers to black township councils. Indeed, the battle to keep order in the townships has undoubtedly become much harder. South Africa is no longer facing a cycle of violence interspersed, as in the past, with long periods of calm. The police are now locked in almost permanent conflict of a kind very different from the three previous waves of black unrest that the National Party (NP) has faced since taking office: the Defiance against Unjust Laws campaign of 1952, the Sharpeville shooting of 1960, and the Soweto uprising of 1976.

The national police force is still remarkably small, with only 45,000 members. Even though the government intends to increase the number to 68,000 by 1993 it may well be inadequate, its training in riot control still rudimentary. The South African Police (SAP) will still have only 3 members per 1,000 of population compared with a Western norm of 6/10. With top instructors in the police colleges already in short supply it is difficult to see how they will be trained or retained once they have left police college. Although enough are coming forward at the moment, any improvement in the economy is bound to affect both recruiting and retention — one reason why some politicians have proposed that national servicemen be allowed to serve in the police force.

From the beginning the police were unable to use the preferred method of containing violence: the use of minimum force – first a show of force on the streets, then the use of nonlethal weapons, from tear gas to rubber bullets – and the use of live ammunition only as a last resort. The large open spaces in the townships, with their high density of population but sprawling geographical mass, did not allow the police to corral the rioters or seal off one sector from another as the police did with conspicuous success in the race riots of the 1960s in the United States. Even the climatic conditions worked against them. The heat and high winds common in the Eastern Cape made it difficult to use tear gas. The degree of aggression shown by the crowds also made classic Ulster-style policing all but impossible; the police were not attempting to separate two factions, or restore order; they themselves were among the principal targets. In the first 16 months of the unrest 35 policemen were murdered and the homes of several hundred more subjected to petrol bombings or other attacks.[12]

Whether the authorities wished it or not, they were forced to rely more than ever on the army, a situation that was clearly foreseeable some years before the present troubles. In 1957 the defense act was specifically amended to allow army units to be used for "the suppression of internal disorder," a task that hitherto had been the sole responsibility of the police. As early as April 1978 the army was mobilized to cordon off the Vaal townships. Despite drawing on its reserve formations, the SAP had to call upon the army to mount 447 road blocks in the three-month period preceding the September 1984 crisis, an operation that was revealed only a year later in an attempt to deflect criticism of the government for using national servicemen in the township rioting.[13] In September the army entered the townships for the first time when 5,000 soldiers joined 2,000 police in a series of house-to-house searches in Seobeng and neighboring areas.

Official government policy regarding army deployments is that, where possible, the SADF should be used only to cordon off black areas, not to enter the townships to restore order, escort delivery vehicles, or protect the lives and property of black policemen and town councillors — activities that have been officially added to its other duties since April 1983. It has also been government policy not to put conscript troops in the front line, especially in situations in which they might have to open fire.[14] Until the state of emergency was temporarily lifted in March 1986, however, soldiers increasingly found themselves conducting house-to-house searches for arms, as well as carrying out arrests and, in some cases, even rounding up truant schoolchildren.

The army is clearly unhappy with this role. In an interview in *Die Suid Afrikaan*, the new commander in chief, Jannie Geldenhuys, insisted that the army's role should be to protect those who need protection, not to arrest political agitators or their supporters:

> It is not the primary task of any army or a defence force. This is not the task for which we were primarily trained. We prefer to be a deterrent. When we have to fight, we want to use tanks and cannon rather than water cannon and plastic shields in internal disturbances.

A number of senior army commanders have argued in private that the use of the army has been not so much uncalculated as miscalculated. At no time, of course, have they totally despaired of the situation; they have no need to. Ultimately they know that if the violence spreads to the white metropolitan areas, they can mobilize up to 1.2 million whites, many of whom have their own firearms (up to 2 million on rough estimates). Having worked together with the police in Namibia, they have learned what *not* to do, even if some of the joint operations have met with indifferent success. Not only do they enjoy better equipment than the rioters, they also have a monopoly of communications and an intelligence network that is far more extensive and sophisticated than that operated by the Rhodesians 10 years ago. If Raymond Aron was right to argue in *The Century of Total War* that what makes modern conflicts different from those of the past is the element of "technical surprise," the generals need feel no misgivings on that score.

But there is no disguising the fact that the army and the police have little confidence in each other. The SAP believes that the standard tactic of all counterinsurgency operations — the gradual escalation of force — is a waste of time and has shown little inclination to implement a classic program of winning the hearts and minds of the population (or WHAM as it is better known in the forces, an acronym the irony of which could only have escaped the South Africans). The general impression one gains from interviewing many senior commanders is that they are largely of the opinion that their counterparts in the police are cut off from reality, cocooned in sectarian self-esteem and intellectual conceit, that they really believe that force can be met with force and that black political leaders will be forced to give way under the momentum of repression.

Most soldiers above the rank of major are not quite aware of the problems they face even in containing the violence at its present level: that most operations are reactive not proactive; that surprise weapons searches have proved useless (as the British army found in Ulster, handguns are easy enough to break up into their constituent parts); and that if the military are facing a siege, not a revolution, there is always the prospect that the blacks may break out into the countryside where the security forces would be seriously overstretched.

In the last resort, policing can only be done by consent. The army, of course, has not yet withheld its consent and shows no immediate signs of doing so, but it is clearly unhappy about its role. At the moment the army may not question the need to intervene, but it does harbor serious reservations about the damage that intervention has done to army morale. It is one sign, certainly an important one, of a society under strain. Since the reform program first began that spectacle has been promised and prophesied by the government's critics on the right, but time and again it has refused to manifest itself. Now it appears to have done so. In its experience of policing the townships, the army seems to have lost its status in its own eyes, and, to that extent, may even have lost some of its confidence too.

What must be most disturbing for the government is the clear reluctance of some senior commanders to become involved in politics on the understanding that this will compromise the army's much prized "political neutrality," a claim that sits somewhat uneasily on its highly political role in the past. The story of civil-military relations after all has not been an especially happy one even for the white community. In 1922 the army, using aircraft and tanks, ruthlessly put down an armed uprising in the Rand – an action in which 200 whites were killed, an insurrection that was far more of a threat to civil order than the 1976 Soweto uprising.

Instead of accepting that "the first task of the armed forces is to help the police maintain law and order," as the country's defense minister insisted in 1963, it has chosen to prepare for a sporadic threat, that of a guerrilla war or total onslaught, a threat that has not yet materialized and probably never will. In reality the challenge the regime faces is endemic, not sporadic: a continuing cycle of internal violence that is not only a threat to the private property of the country's population but also to the divide and rule strategy at the heart of the reform program.

As the loss of property mounts and the Republic becomes even more isolated internationally so the authority of the state that the army is pledged to serve will be relentlessly eroded. If violence is perceived to be endemic and unmanageable, any black support Pretoria may be able to count upon will soon vanish. The blacks will simply refuse to cooperate in any schemes the government initiates – a fact that will mark not so much an endgame as a refusal to play the game any longer.

Citizens in Arms

The country's political leaders have also begun to voice general misgivings about the morale of conscript troops. Ever increasing rates of desertion and evasion of the draft have added to a picture of widespread dissatisfaction about the terms of national service, a vital element in the SADF's strength. Ten years ago only 2.9 percent of South Africa's total ground forces, both active duty and reserve, were full-time, professional soldiers. A manpower structure with a professional component of only 6 percent and trained full-time units of only 17 percent of the defense force was clearly inadequate. The 1977 white paper on defense was highly critical of the government for relying so heavily on conscript soldiers, particularly in the field.

Even today South Africa has one of the lowest rates of voluntary military service in the world. In 1979 the Defense Ministry reported a critical shortage of instructors and a 20 percent shortfall in the number of noncommissioned officers and pilots. Those numbers have not been made good. Even in the rural areas the situation is little better, which suggests that the material attraction of city life is not the only explanation for a reluctance to join up. At the moment, 37 percent of the rural commandos are undermanned. Mounting casualty rates have had a marked, notably adverse impact on recruitment for what was originally an all-volunteer force.[15]

Inevitably, recent events have resulted in much tougher terms of national service. The period that conscripts are now required to serve in the Citizen Force has increased from 240 days over 8 years to 720 days over 12, a three-fold increase. Requests for exemption have risen equally dramatically. Of 59,052 men who were called up in 1977 no less than 32,095 successfully obtained exemption or deferment.[16] The 15 to 35-year-old labor pool happens, of course, to account for 40 percent of the Republic's economically active white workers, yet if the manpower needs of the economy are real enough this still does not explain why evasion rates are quite so high. Possibly as many as 25 percent of all those mobilized in any year evade the call-up. Evasion of military service is one thing, refusal to serve quite another. In an attempt to recruit an additional 2,000 men every year a new citizenship bill, which became law in October 1984, tried to net recent immigrants. Instead it has merely encouraged emigration, with 140 families now leaving every month. Every year since the 1976 uprising an estimated 3–4,000 whites have also failed to turn up for the draft. Hundreds have been imprisoned; thousands more have fled the country altogether, applying for political asylum or refugee status in Britain, the Netherlands, or the United States.

Ever since troops were deployed in the townships the numbers have increased dramatically, an interesting, perhaps telling statement of white support for the existing order. Serving in Namibia may be one thing, a senseless gesture in support of a cause long lost; refusing to enforce white supremacy at home reveals a highly equivocal attitude toward white supremacy. In the main, such elite troops as the No. I Parachute Battalion were not committed to the townships until March 1986, after 20 months of uninterrupted violence. By contrast, conscripts were sent in early not only to seal off the townships, but also to protect the property of black councillors and police and guard food convoys in the worst affected areas.

Inevitably this has had an adverse effect on morale. The army is not the best instrument for policing. Its weapons are designed to kill, not disarm. In the early days of the unrest some army units were deliberately disarmed for fear that their mere presence might incite violence. Inevitably, the soldiers have found themselves cast in the role of an auxiliary police force, a role that has diminished their public credibility and undermined any claim to political neutrality among the black population. In these circumstances the anticonscription movement has thrived. The decision of the Progressive Federal Party to oppose the use of conscript troops in the townships has provided additional "respectability" to the campaign.

In 1985, 7,000 young men failed to turn up for the call-up—about 40 percent of those mobilized. Although the authorities have since argued that almost all were students and, therefore, would have qualified for deferment, that still leaves unanswered the question of whether they will all agree to be drafted. Recent surveys carried out in four of the Republic's main English-speaking universities—Durban, Cape Town, Rhodes, and the Witwatersrand—have shown that up to two-thirds of all students regard military service with distaste and service in Namibia as illegal.

In any other society such opposition could be written off as an attitude to be expected of young men from a materialistic social environment who, cushioned from hardship most of their lives, could hardly be expected to relish the prospect of spending 24 months or longer in military uniform, especially in an army notorious for its ill-treatment of conscript soldiers. Clearly, many have no stomach for leaving the comfort of the towns for the harsh and inhospitable environment of Namibia. In South Africa, however, draft dodging is more significant than in any other country because of the political implications that logically follow from it.

It must never be forgotten that only those who exercise political power are required by the state to serve in the armed forces. Less than 10 percent of the SADF is made up of nonwhite volunteers, those who are not the beneficiaries of white supremacy. During his two years in the ranks the enlisted citizen is, therefore, more than a conscript soldier serving under duress. He is an integral member of what has been called "the white electorate in arms."[17] As the 1973 white paper on defense argued with compelling logic,

> Defence is not a matter for the defence force alone but also for each . . . citizen; it demands dedication, vigilance and sacrifice . . . from all who are privileged to find a home in this country.[18]

It follows that draft dodging, desertion in the field, evasion of military service, even the refusal of more than 16 of the Cape's 215 civic municipalities to draw up "effective" civil defense programs reflect more than traditional civilian dislike of military service. It is an implicit criticism of a society that requires only those who have the vote to join up.

Certainly, as one of the enduring elements in the power of the state the army is beginning to look a little less durable than it once did. There may, indeed, be every reason to question the traditional assumption that "of all social structures the army is the last intact group in a disintegrating society."[19] Such a claim may be as misleading of South Africa as it has proved to be almost everywhere else.

On the Frontier

Beyond the townships and South Africa's industrial heartland in the rural areas of the north, morale also seems to be crumbling. Here the security situation may be less daunting, but it happens to be more immediate for the white population. In the first six months of 1985 there were as many attacks by the ANC on rural targets as in the whole of the previous year. To meet this challenge the SADF has come to rely on a point defense system on the frontier that is modeled on the system used by the Israeli settlements in the Negev desert to cope with localized infiltration and low-intensity threats. Under the terms of the 1982 defense act, a total of six districts on or near South Africa's border with Swaziland and Mozambique have been activated for "area defense."[20]

Unlike the situation in Israel, however, there seems to be a disquieting reluctance on the part of many white farmers to play the role allotted to them. A committee that investigated border security in 1979 discovered that no less than 44 percent of the farms surveyed had no white tenants. In one district in the northeast Transvaal the numbers were down to 20 percent.[21] This situation has gravely alarmed the country's military leaders who are well aware that in Rhodesia the integration of the farming communities in the "Agric-Alert" communications system played a vital role in providing the security forces with early warning of guerrilla movements.

The result is that at present a guerrilla unit can march from the Limpopo river through to Pietersburg (100 miles south of Zimbabwe) without having to set foot on a farm occupied by whites. The situation with the farmers is one in which security has already begun to break down, the state can no longer defend its citizens, and some are already beginning to think in terms of a new order. It is the classic situation of a system of security that has lost its last and strongest support: fear of the unknown. If the government should ever try to regroup its forces it is by no means clear how many would follow its lead.

Neither financial incentives nor punitive measures appear able to halt the exodus. Neither interest-free nor low-interest loans for young men with military experience willing to take up farming in the areas most under threat, or the new rules introduced in May 1983 requiring people buying or renting farms to remain *in situ* for 300 days a year, seem to have stemmed the flood. In April 1985 the authorities stepped up their attempt to keep farmers on the strategically important borders with Botswana and Zimbabwe by declaring a 5-mile wide strip a special "designated area," a zone in which farmers were given additional financial assistance to stay or settle. Later the area was extended from 5 miles to 30; any farmer who accepts the aid, but subsequently departs, faces a fine of as much as R5,000 or five years in prison.

In many areas, of course, the explanation for white absenteeism has little to do with security fears but much more with high operating costs and the scarcity of arable land. At the end of 1984 their debt amounted to R9.5 billion, 374 percent up on the 1975 figure. High interest rates, 3 percent higher than an already unprecedented annual rate of inflation, have driven many farmers out of business and made absentee landlords of many others. Yet the government can hardly draw much comfort from this fact. If farmers are leaving because of economic hardship they are hardly likely to brave military hazards when they come. More to the point, perhaps, the farming community is becoming more ambivalent in its attitude toward apartheid. As its interests have changed so it has become increasingly sensitive to the economic as well as the military costs of continued white rule.

Previously the farmers were among the most outspoken supporters of a system that not only confirmed their title to land, but also protected them from black competition and provided them with abundant cheap labor. Today apartheid has become largely irrelevant to their position. At the beginning of the 1980s they joined with the businessmen of Natal to draft the Lombard Report, which argued that separate development no longer promised stable government; indeed, that stability demanded the emergence of "new legitimate political institutions that allowed the effective participation of the governed." The report went on to recommend a major experiment in power sharing, a conclusion that met with widespread endorsement in the farming community except in some pockets of the notoriously conservative Transvaal. Many farmers are convinced, rightly or wrongly, that the prospect of food shortages of the kind that have bedeviled most other independent black states will persuade a future black government to treat them as a special case, if not a privileged community. The cooperation agreement between the Zulus and Afrikaner farmers at Louwsburg in August 1986 provides a significant example of local accommodation of the kind just discussed.[22]

Such attitudes relentlessly test simple models of black-white opposition. In a sense "the alibi of the past," to quote V. S. Naipaul, is no longer enough. "The past has vanished. Facts in a book cannot by themselves give people a sense of history.[23] In the Afrikaner collective consciousness, memories of the Great Trek and Blood River probably count for much less than more recent memories of the 1930s and the years of acute agricultural depression, which have been rekindled by three successive years of drought. Insofar as the 20 percent of Afrikaners who still live on the land face a threat, it has taken the form not of a guerrilla war but of run-down personal savings and a growing accumulation of personal debt.

In circumstances in which 40 percent of all farms on the border with Zimbabwe are at present lying unoccupied, in addition to 45 percent on the border with Botswana and 15 percent on that with Mozambique, there is hardly much scope for the idea proposed by the former deputy defense minister, Kobie Coetzee, for settling war veterans in a chain of defense strongholds along outlying districts on the frontier. For many farmers, though by no means all, the state, not the ANC, has become the main threat to their continued livelihood. We might even go further and suggest that the quickening unrest within South Africa has begun to blur the meaning of the frontier altogether. It certainly seems to be shifting all the time. Of the land area of the Republic, much of it adjacent to major metropolitan areas, 13 percent is divided into homelands, some with their own private armies that would still rely on the SADF for most of their training and equipment.

A problem of major proportions might arise were a homeland such as Venda, which has been "independent" since 1978, to dissolve into disorder. In Transkei, the eastern Pondoland disturbances in September 1983 had to be suppressed by the defense force, not the police. In the same month, the citizens of Grahamstown and Williamstown were required to register for immediate service in the reserves when it looked as if Ciskei, another homeland, might be about to collapse.[24] For years, white farmers living on the frontier with such "states" have also lived with the prospect of being called up to seal them off or even intervene to restore a semblance of order. Apparently it remains as true today as it did 10 years ago that the defense of the homelands is an inherent part of local defense, that they still occupy a position within "the military milieu of the RSA and not outside" it, in P. W. Botha's own words.[25]

In 1986 increasing emphasis was placed on "area defense." The Military Area Radio Network, an emergency radio communications system designed specifically to provide communications and alarm facilities for both civilians and military commandos in remote or sensitive areas, is part of a general plan to enhance the country's state of alert in the event of a rural revolt. Despite this contingency planning the military know full well that the manpower at their disposal would be grossly inadequate to cope with a rural revolt like that in Pondoland in 1961, the long-forgotten disturbances that followed in the wake of Sharpeville.

The threat of rural unrest should be taken seriously. As a revolutionary movement the ANC is committed to the typical revolutionary broad-front strategy of expanding the current urban unrest farther afield where it will be much harder to contain and deal with. Its political literature envisages a mobile campaign in which larger units armed with advanced weapons will carry out lightening attacks against the enemy. At this stage mobile warfare will be translated into positional warfare with liberated zones in the countryside encircling the cities, even the autonomous metropolitan areas that the government seems intent on establishing in the near future.[26]

The example of the Pondoland revolt in the early 1960s offers the army a salutary warning of the form and scope that rural violence might take. One of the significant factors of the 1961 uprising was the speed and manner in which it moved beyond acts of uncoordinated violence into a general rebellion against the authority of the local chiefdoms in Transkei. Another was that far from representing a pallid reflection of the urbanized uprising at Sharpeville on which it closely followed, the unrest developed a specific rationale of its own. In the end the government was forced to arrest more than 5,000 people, slightly more than a third of the number detained in South Africa as a whole during the second state of emergency in 1986. Thousands of especially trained riot police aided by heavily armed troops with helicopter support were called in to crush the rebellion. To deal with this kind of violence in the future, the kind that prevented the homeland government of KwaNdebele from seeking independence in the summer of 1986, the army may intend persuading the local communities to police the regions themselves, thereby decentralizing military power without relinquishing overall control.

The Lombard Report (1980) originally envisaged dividing the country into eight separate zones. Although at no time has the government indicated any willingness to pursue its recommendations to the letter, recent developments do indicate that regionalization of a kind is already being pursued, albeit by stealth, perhaps even unconsciously. If Natal and KwaZulu merge into a semi-autonomous federation, the East London area may combine in a similar arrangement with Ciskei and Transkei. Similar experiments might be followed up with other homelands, some of which have security forces of their own, which would be one way of "Africanizing" the security forces while not actually diluting the white element in the national army, a point to which many members of the military would be clearly opposed.

Although there is no homeland in the Cape province with which local white communities can come to an arrangement, it is significant that command and provincial boundaries have begun to overlap for the first time in the country's history and that the Western Cape Command now corresponds almost exactly to the Western Province Industrial Development Area. One of the little noticed guidelines of the proposed nominated provincial councils is that they will have the power to redraw provincial boundaries without seeking prior government approval, presumably redrawing military command areas at the same time.

Indeed, the border areas within South Africa are already beginning to remind one of the outlying provinces of the later Roman Empire, its citizens waiting expectantly for barbarians to appear on the horizon, largely oblivious to the presence among them of outsiders who arrived unnoticed many generations before. The war at home is taking on new immediacy. In the industrial heartland of South Africa 30-day call-ups for national servicemen have been doubled. Members of the Citizen Force can now be called up for 60 days of continuous service; outside the country they are still only required to see active service for 90 days in alternate years.

Whether these developments should be seen in an entirely negative light is another matter. Like the barbarians of Cavafy's poem the phenomenon may provide a solution, releasing the republic from "the jagged time of rise and fall, of beginning and end, of catastrophe," blurring the chronology of disaster from the time power is held to the time it is finally transferred.[27]

3

Limits of the *Pax Pretoriana*

> Dr. Johnson: Sir, what is all this rout about the Corsi-
> cans? They have been at war with the Genoese for up-
> wards of twenty years and have never yet taken their
> fortified towns. They might have pulled the walls in
> pieces with their teeth in twenty years.
> — Felix Markham, *Napoleon*

Like Operation Blitz One in September 1977, Operation
Thunder Chariot, an exercise held in September 1984, was
designed to test a mechanized combat group in conventional warfare.[28] Compared with the 1950s and 1960s when the
SADF had planned for a general war in which its own forces
might be sent overseas as they had in two world wars and
Korea, the intervention of Cuban troops in Angola concen-
trated the military mind on the possibility of a conventional
war along South Africa's own borders, a threat that came to
be described in the government's own publications as a "total onslaught." Acting on the worst case premise, military
bases were constructed along the borders with Botswana
and Mozambique, a new brigade school was established at
Sishen in the Kalahari, and plans were developed for a 6-
mile deep "free fire zone" along the entire length of the frontier. There was even talk of relocating some of the industrial

centers between the Cape, Durban, and Pinetown in the hope that a geographically dispersed economic war machine would be more difficult to attack.[29]

Even today it is still not clear how seriously the South Africans took either the threat or the strategy that was devised to deal with it. It is certainly true that as late as 1982 the defense white paper argued trenchantly that "the presence of Soviet armaments in the neighbouring countries of the republic of South Africa (RSA) . . . increases the possibility of a conventional threat to the republic and South-West Africa even in the short or medium term," an assessment that was far more pessimistic, even alarmist, than most. The apparently unstoppable influx of Soviet arms into the area alarmed the generals and politicians alike. By the end of 1983, on the calculations of South African Defense Minister General Magnus Malan, the USSR had supplied more than $15 billion to the Frontline States (FLS) in the previous five years. Yet many generals were prepared to admit in private that the input of military hardware as such had not been especially significant, that it had done little to change the military equation in the FLS's favor, or that it had served to dissuade the South Africans themselves from attacking such close Soviet clients as Angola or Mozambique.

The total onslaught had begun to sound increasingly hollow by the end of 1983. An editorial in the South African army journal, *Paratus*, compared it with a coin that had been devalued through excessive handling: "The term 'total onslaught' had lost currency because some people feel that it has been overexposed and overused." According to John Seiler, in a secret directive to senior SADF commanders that summer the strategy was finally downgraded. On Malan's direct instructions all mention of the term was dropped from army courses except from the advanced interdepartmental joint course at the Defense Staff College.

Yet the removal of the most serious threat has not improved South Africa's position significantly. It is still faced with an open-ended and apparently unending war in Nami-

bia, now more than 17 years old, with the prospect of continued low level infiltration along its borders by the ANC,
and with the cost of the permanent perimeter deployment
of its forces. Although the total onslaught has been downgraded, the problem of defense against external attack has
not disappeared. The problem is largely structural rather
than strategic: what can South Africa afford at a minimum
cost to itself? The republic may have several geographic
advantages, including extensive internal lines of communication, the best in southern Africa, but it has insufficient
forces to man a defense perimeter permanently.

The SADF had only 34,400 regular troops in 1985, only
3,000 more than in 1975, of which 8,400 were in the army.
The rest were conscript soldiers. The defense white paper of
1975 complained at length that the officer corps was so
understrength that it was moving rapidly toward what it
described as a "potential danger point." Ten years later the
SADF is still 20 percent short of officers and NCOs, even
more critically so of trained pilots. It still has one of the
lowest volunteer rates of any major armed force in the
world.

All national servicemen are of course required to serve
for two years in the ranks. From there they are put on an
active reserve known as the Citizen Force, 130,000 strong,
where they can expect to spend a total of 720 days in uniform over a period of 12 years. Even the Permanent Force
cannot undertake operations unless the Citizen Force is mobilized, an obvious constraint on combat operations. Regular call-ups for day-to-day operations would be disastrous
for an economy that is already critically short of trained
manpower. The problem is compounded by the fact that
only 22 percent of military manpower is actually required
for combat operations. Every national serviceman in the
field requires three or more men in a supporting role.[30]

Accordingly, the SADF has been forced to eliminate the
need for continuous frontier defense, to maximize its net
disposable power, to engage the enemy not on the border
but well beyond it. Since the late 1970s the South Africans

have adopted a mobile offensive form of defense rather than a static defensive mode of operations – a strategy that the Israelis describe as one of "anticipatory counterattacks," but one that South African commanders prefer to call "a protracted war of low intensity" or "offensive pro-active action."[31]

Fifty years ago the veteran South African leader Jan Smuts recognized that if the Republic were to be defended at all "it would have to proceed at a great distance beyond its frontier, the only question being how far beyond." In those days, of course, the question tended to be more rhetorical than real. Today it is asked increasingly often.

Since 1978 the SADF has succeeded in dealing with the threat of insurgency not by manning the frontier but by taking the war to the FLS. In December 1985 the Angolan government cited 4,000 intrusions into Angolan airspace since 1981, as well as 168 bombing missions, 234 airborne troop landings, 74 ground attacks, and 7 full-scale "invasions," somewhat euphemistically described as raids in the international press. The policy has not been inexpensive. Not only has it accounted for an ever increasing share of the defense budget – no less than 73 percent in 1983–1984, it has also required the most extensive mobilization of the country's forces since World War II. The real question is whether it has been especially effective in the two countries in which it has been applied most consistently – Angola and Mozambique. And what of Namibia, where South African forces have been engaged in a protracted and expensive struggle that has so far cost the lives of 560 South African soldiers on the government's calculations, possibly considerably more?[32]

If we take the security typology developed by the British scholar Barry Buzan, South Africa clearly fits the model of a strong regional power but a weak state whose political institutions and prevailing political ideology are rejected by all but a minority of its citizens. Buzan concludes that all such powers should address their internal threats, not look for causes of conflict beyond their own frontiers.[33] If we look at the three case studies cited, this would appear to be especially true of South Africa.

Angola, 1978–1986

The strategy of preemptive attack had its origins in a warning by John Vorster as long ago as 1967, directed at Zambia for its decision to allow the South-West Africa People's Organization (SWAPO) to use the country as a base for its own operations. Writing only a few years later, Kenneth Grundy correctly foresaw that only a narrow dividing line distinguished military action from political intervention.[34] That line was first crossed in Angola in 1975 during Operation Savannah, "the first occasion in 30 years," according to the South African army newspaper, *Paratus*, "that large numbers of South African troops had gone into action in a situation resembling conventional war."

Operation Reindeer three years later was the first in a long series of clashes between the Angolan army and the SADF. Operation Smokeshell in 1980 was the most extensive to date, involving three squadrons of Mirage and Buccanneer aircraft that might have tipped the balance in Pretoria's favor had they been committed in 1975. Operation Protea the following year, one of three "raids" in 1981, was even larger, drawing on 11,000 men and more than 250 armored vehicles, including 90 Centurion tanks.

By putting the Angolans permanently on the defensive South Africa was able to maximize its limited manpower. It needed to. Even in 1980 the SWAPO threat in Namibia tied down 25,000 men even though the guerrillas in the field never numbered more than 2,000. The rest were seconded to the Angolan armed forces to fight the National Union for the Total Independence of Angola (UNITA) or to guard the southern railway lines against rebel attack. The sheer scale of counterinsurgency operations, even against an enemy force much reduced in numbers, explains why South Africa's commanders have never been enthusiastic about reduc-

Map 1
ANGOLA

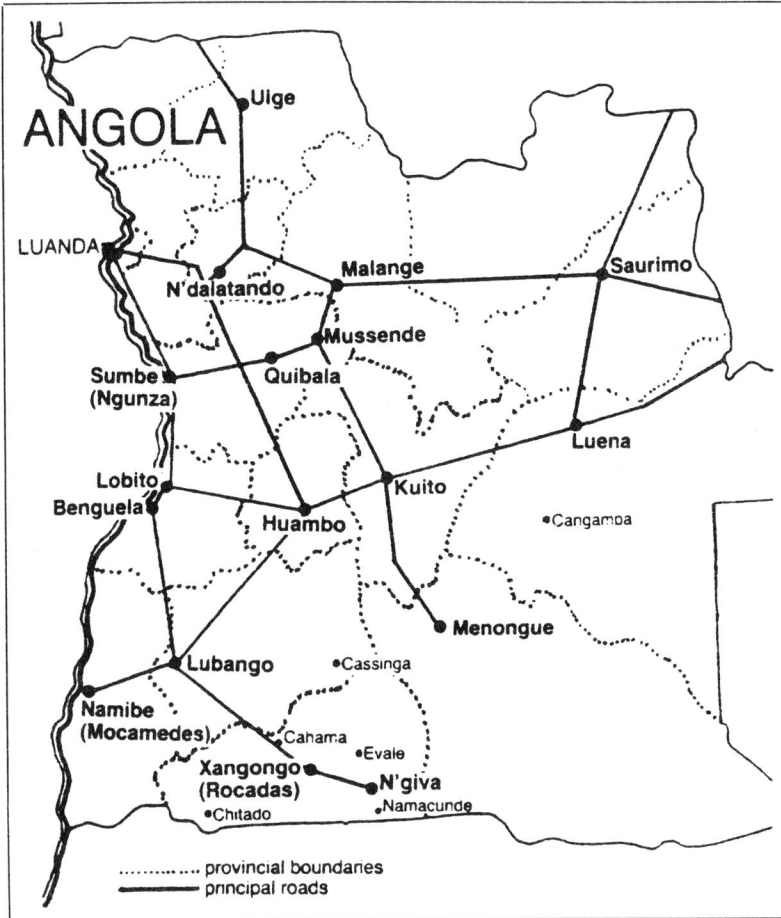

ing the Republic's defense perimeter, defending familiar ground, and exploiting short, interior lines of communication. In other words, they have never been particularly outspoken in their support of a policy of strategic retrenchment in all but name. The manpower for such a strategy simply does not exist, even on paper. It would be erroneous, however, to imagine that the SADF's existing policy has met with unqualified success or that the army has not suffered serious reverses. The military balance has begun to shift against the Republic in at least three respects, the last of which may yet prove decisive.

First, the Angolans are now better trained and better equipped than they have been for many years. Improved performance in the field owes a great deal to the combined efforts of Cuban and Soviet training and Soviet supplied equipment. Eighty percent of all combat missions by the Angolan airforce are now flown by Angolan pilots, compared to 40 percent three years ago.[35] In short, the last few years have witnessed some success in the slow and often painful process of converting an ill-disciplined guerrilla force into a regular army able to hold its own against the SADF. The results may have been mixed, but they have not been unimpressive.

Operation Protea was halted in the summer of 1981 by Angolan resistance at Cahama, with the result that the front line was established a few kilometers south of the town. It was an impressive achievement given that the invading force consisted of 11,000 men, with M-41 and Centurion tanks and Ferret, Saracen, and Ratel armored cars. During another raid the same year, the South Africans failed to capture Menongue, the capital of Kuando Kubango, despite a diversionary attack on Luanda that was intended to prevent the Angolan army from sending reinforcements to the town.

Even Operation Askari (December 1983) ended in such high losses that the SADF was forced to withdraw some days ahead of schedule. It now seems clear that the Angolan 11th Brigade gave a good account of itself, preventing the capture of three important towns.[36] Askari in particular highlighted a number of operational failures for which there was little if any excuse, including inadequate counter-battery fire at Cuvelai. The army was also surprised when, instead of using its tank force as dug-in artillery, one Angolan armored brigade managed for the first time to break through the SADF's fixed positions without losing a single vehicle. With 40 armored vehicles and 5 (possibly 6) Mirage aircraft brought down in the attack, according to a report in *Africa Confidential*, South Africa's strategic retreat may well have marked if not the limits of its operational capacity, the end of such free-ranging operations as Daisy (1981), when its forces penetrated 250 km inland largely unchallenged.

Second, the Angolans have been helped in their resistance by a marked improvement in the quality of their weapons. Prior to Smokeshell or Askari, the South Africans were not able to rearm, as did the Israelis prior to their 1982 invasion of Lebanon when the delivery of U.S. equipment was 50 percent higher than in previous years. Angola has been more fortunate. During its own offensive against Jonas Savimbi in the autumn of 1985 it was able to deploy 71 aircraft, including such advanced models as the MiG-23 and SU-22 supersonic bomber. The 11 brigades stationed at Mavinga were able to call upon 30 tanks and more than 80 armored vehicles, most of them recently supplied by Moscow.

P. W. Botha was clearly conscious of the ebbing military advantage when he warned the West at the time that unless the situation was soon redressed South Africa could not hope to compete on equal terms.[37] The SADF has only 250 main battle tanks, divided between two separate tank battalions and two divisions on three separate fronts. A NATO tank division has 324 tanks, a Warsaw Pact division slightly more. In other words, South Africa's tank strength is not particularly impressive, especially when it is recalled that up to 20 percent of any armored force may be immobilized by mechanical failure en route to the field of battle. In the combat conditions in which the SADF has to operate, this is probably far more worrying for its commanders than the prospect of the high attrition rates incurred by the two opposing forces during the last Arab-Israeli conflict.

The air force is also strikingly in need of more modern aircraft. Over half of its Mirages are grounded because of a shortage of spare parts and equipment. Its few Impala squadrons are rotated through the three main airbases on the Angolan border every three months.[38] As for its bombers, most of the Buccaneers have either crashed or been cannibalized for spare parts. It now has to rely almost entirely on Mirage F-1 and F-IIIs, which although considerably more versatile are now 24 years old.

None of these deficiencies necessarily detracts from the abilities of the South African Air Force's (SAAF) pilots, which were clearly demonstrated in 1985 during Angola's abortive offensive against UNITA. In the course of the fighting they succeeded in strafing 15 helicopters and 6 aircraft on the ground, thus effectively blunting the attack. At the moment, South Africa's air supremacy is real enough. Zimbabwe's air force, like that of Mozambique, is for all practical purposes nonoperational, which limits the combat matchup to Angola where the SAAF's Mirages have to face mostly MiG-21s, occasionaly MiG-23s. Actually, the comparison between the Mirage IIICZ and the Angolan MiG-23s is somewhat misleading, because the latter are Flogger Fs assigned to ground-attack units. With little air-to-air capability, they would not survive an encounter with a Mirage for long. Even if the Flogger E, which *is* designed for aerial combat, were to be imported the differences would be only marginally in Angola's favor and could easily be offset by a South African pilot who was 20 percent more proficient than his Angolan counterpart.

Third, the principal reason South Africa has lost its margin of superiority in the last 24 months has been the Soviet Union's belated response to its own strategy of "proactive action." Pretoria was, in that respect, extremely fortunate that the raids into Angola did not provoke Moscow much earlier. Under the leadership of Leonid Brezhnev and his immediate successors the USSR was clearly reluctant to become involved in the kind of undeclared air war that preceded the Yom Kippur war. Even when the Soviet ambassador at the UN delivered a stern warning to Pretoria in the wake of Operation Askari he was careful to insist that it should not be construed as a "threat," only a forecast of the "logical and reasonable consequences" of South Africa's conduct.[39] Significantly, the consequences were not spelled out. Once the USSR realized that the raids had become an end in themselves, not a means to an end, the expression not of a *Pax Pretoriana* but a permanent cycle of instability, they began to intervene much more decisively on Luanda's behalf.

The construction of a Soviet air umbrella in the south — more than 1,500 antiaircraft weapons and 800 surface-to-air missiles (SAMs) — has left South Africa only the extreme southeast of Angola in which to operate.[40] Although the majority of SAMs were old SA-7s, in 1986 Moscow provided its principal ally in the region, Angola, with the largest and most varied collection of SAMs, radar, and communications south of Syria. Angola indeed was the first country outside the Warsaw Pact to receive SA-9s. The deployment of SA-8s seems to have determined the outcome of the fighting at Cahama and Cuvelai in December 1983, in the course of which five Mirages were shot down, some at ranges of 20 km and over. During the operation the SAAF suffered the highest attrition rate of any raid since June 1980 when it lost four Impalas to a combination of ground fire and SA-7s. There used to be a time when South African pilots could expect to face 57 SAMs every mission; today the number is probably as high as 90, a rate of antiaircraft fire even more intense than that which the SAAF experienced in Korea.

The success with which UNITA managed to attack the Angolan stronghold of Cuito Cuanaval in August 1986 (the first time that it had gone on to the offensive for some time), allegedly assisted by a substantial detachment of South African troops, was only made possible because Savimbi was able to use his U.S.-supplied Stinger missiles to great effect. Up to 11 aircraft, mostly MiG-21s and Mi-25 helicopter gunships, were brought down in the first week of the operation, so many that the Angolan air force is believed to have refused several days later to provide air sup-

port for its own troops on the ground because of the danger
to its own aircraft. The Stinger missiles have for the moment at least provided a "permissive environment" in which
the SADF can now operate without relying on air-to-ground
support of its own.

If the air umbrella is extended any further, however, the
situation could change decisively. Immediately before the
1985 offensive, the retiring chief of the SADF, General Viljoen, warned that the Soviet buildup could easily "tip the
scales" in Angola's favor: "A disparity in the strength of
airpower in favour of the republic's hostile neighbours could
limit reprisals against terrorist bases in neighbouring countries."[41] At the same time chief of the SAAF Lieutenant
General Dennis Earp warned that the Soviet air umbrella,
although less extensive, was as formidable as that in the
Middle East:

> As the air umbrella is becoming more effective it is
> obvious that it is becoming more difficult to neutralise.
> . . . And unless it is neutralised no long range opera-
> tions are possible without heavy casualties.[42]

There could be no more telling warning that the days of
SAAF superiority in the air may be limited, if not fast
disappearing, with all that this might mean for South Africa's present strategy of preemption.

Mozambique, 1981–1986

The policy of destabilization, as we have seen, was originally intended to spare South Africa the expense of patroling a
long *cordon sanitaire*. By concentrating its forces on both
sides of the frontier when circumstances required, it did not
need to so much to occupy any territory as to deny control
to the opposing side. This was precisely the policy it followed in Mozambique. On taking over the MNR on the eve
of the Lancaster House conference in 1979, the South Africans trained the movement to strike at economic targets as

Map 2

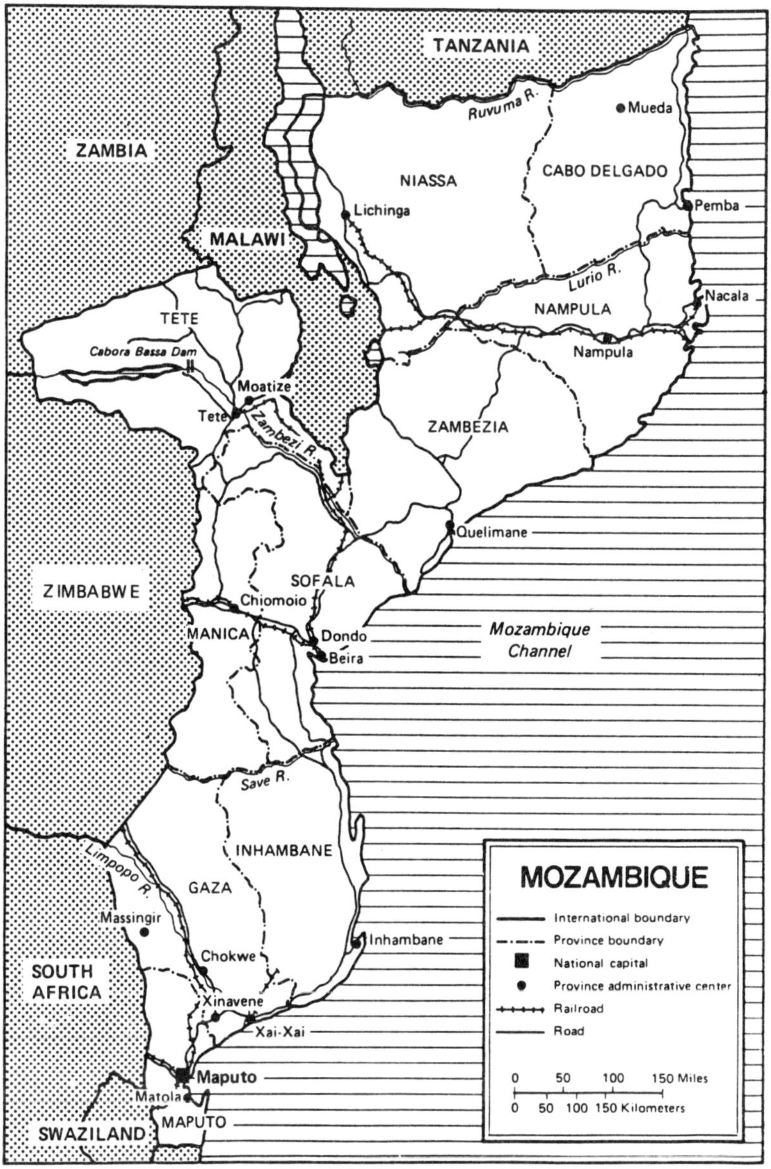
TANZANIA
ZAMBIA
MALAWI
ZIMBABWE
SOUTH AFRICA
SWAZILAND
Ruvuma R.
Mueda
CABO DELGADO
NIASSA
Lichinga
Pemba
Lurio R.
Nacala
NAMPULA
Nampula
TETE
Cabora Bassa Dam
Moatize
Tete
Zambezi R.
ZAMBEZIA
Quelimane
SOFALA
Chiomoio
MANICA
Dondo
Beira
Mozambique Channel
Save R.
INHAMBANE
Limpopo R.
GAZA
Massingir
Chokwe
Inhambane
Xinavene
Xai-Xai
Maputo
Matola
MAPUTO
MOZAMBIQUE
International boundary
Province boundary
National capital
Province administrative center
Railroad
Road
0 50 100 150 Miles
0 50 100 150 Kilometers

far as the suburbs of Beira. From time to time, notably in
1981 and 1983, the SADF also launched attacks against
ANC facilities on the outskirts of Maputo. By the end of
1983 Mozambique had incurred $3 billion damage from the
economic deprivations of an especially disruptive guerrilla
campaign sponsored and directed by Pretoria.

Although South Africa succeeded in forcing the government of Samora Machel to sign the Nkomati agreement,
it has since found it much more difficult to keep the peace.
Indeed, for all the talk of a *Pax Pretoriana*, far from representing a peace, Pretoria seems only to have created an
endemic state of insecurity for the protecting power as well
as its clients. South Africa may dispose of sufficient military power to force its neighbors to sign nonaggression
pacts, but once they are signed it cannot police them. Even
if it wished, it cannot defend local regimes against movements such as the MNR, which it has itself sustained for
many years. In short, it cannot decide the extent to which
the FLS can absorb their own insecurity.

This is clearly the case in Mozambique where before the
Nkomati accord the MNR was active in 7 out of the country's 10 provinces. Maputo signed the agreement because it
believed South African support for the rebels would be
withdrawn. By the end of 1985, however, the number of
contacts between the security forces and the guerrillas was
averaging 130 a month compared to 70 before Nkomati—85
percent of them initiated by the MNR against an under-
paid, underequipped, undertrained army that by then was
capable only of defending the capital and the major cities.

Contrary to popular belief, not all members of the
South African government were determined to undermine
the Nkomati agreement even though many members of the
SADF were far from sympathetic with all of its aims. Pretoria provided Machel with vehicles and equipment worth R4
million, on a scale far more impressive than the $1 million of
nonlethal supplies provided by the United States. It even
proposed joint patrols along the Ressano-Garcia Maputo
road and offered to send reconnaissance flights over the

Cabora Bassa powerline to facilitate its defense against rebel attacks. In a further attempt to salvage the Nkomati accord the government declared the frontier with Mozambique a "special restricted air space." By December 1984 the number of airdrops to the MNR from South Africa had fallen to two compared with eight from Malawi.[43] The security forces set up a chain of radar stations to detect low-flying aircraft and established a joint monitoring team on the border. They stopped short, however, of armed intervention on Machel's behalf.

The problem was that South Africa could not police Nkomati itself. Although P. W. Botha promised to consider military intervention "on merit" after receiving representations to this effect from the U.S. and British governments, the SADF had too few troops to launch a sweep through the province of Manica as the Zimbabwean army did in the Tete that summer.[44] At one point, 17 percent of the Zimbabwean army was deployed in Mozambique, patroling the vital Beira-Mutare corridor with its oil and rail links. All that the South Africans have to spare are members of the 4,000 strong, 32nd Battalion who have moved into position on the border, ready to intervene in an emergency. The government can hardly ask conscript forces to serve in yet another theater of operations, especially in defense of a regime that has been portrayed for years in the press as being beyond the pale of civilized conduct.

Far from policing Nkomati, the South Africans have stood on the sidelines watching their own economic influence being progressively undermined. The road and rail links from South Africa to Maputo, which used to carry 6 million tons of South African goods before independence, now carry fewer than 1 million. The rail link from Beira to Zimbabwe, 180 km away, is actually safer because of the presence of the Zimbabwean army. Responsibility for the defense of the rail link to Maputo remains that of the South African Transport Services, not the SADF.

The same is even true of the Cabora Bassa power line. Within six weeks of Nkomati, the Electricity Supply Commission (ESCOM) agreed to pay 50 percent more for electricity from the dam, thereby increasing the value of the South African link. Yet since October 1983, when the MNR sabotaged 27 of the 6,400 pylons between Chimoio and Gogoi, more than 500 km from the dam itself, no power has actually been supplied. Although ESCOM has recruited security guards to protect the grid, most of the power lines have been sabotaged almost as soon as they have been repaired. In short, South Africa has not succeeded in constructing a viable security system. Its client states are not clients at all. Pretoria does not have the forces to keep them under control or even to help them deal with internal opposition. We may be dealing with an economy of force but not of political power; South Africa's political influence is strictly limited. There is no geographic depth to its defense; in some cases it has merely driven the FLS even farther into the Soviet orbit.

The destabilization of South Africa's neighbors will, in the future, probably have no other object than sanctions busting, appropriately enough carried out by nonmilitary means. Force may have demonstrably failed as a political instrument either to create a security system acceptable to Pretoria or even to reduce the FLS to abject submission. The South Africans will still be able to contribute to the further dissolution of Zimbabwe or Mozambique, however, simply by flexing their economic muscle—placing hurdles in the way of transit goods, closing the border, reducing foreign labor, cutting electricity, and suspending credit facilities altogether. "Negative destabilization" would not require the use of the army at all; the same ends could be achieved by different methods.

Where neighboring countries may seek to weaken the South African economy by seeking different outlets to the sea, force probably will be used, though more selectively than in the past. The Beira-Mutare corridor could be rendered inoperable within days if the port of Beira were put out of commission. This could be engineered without much difficulty by special operation squadrons based in Natal, which are already involved in reconnaissance missions in Niassa and therefore more than familiar with the locale.

Namibia, 1965–

The year 1986 marked the twenty-first anniversary of the war in South-West Africa, a guerrilla campaign with the dubious distinction of being the least successful national liberation struggle this century militarily, despite widespread international support and substantial financial backing. The Soviet Union is clearly exasperated that the movement has made so little progress, indeed that it is finding it increasingly difficult to recruit new members, even among the Ovambo, its principal tribal base. At times

Map 3
NORTHERN NAMIBIA

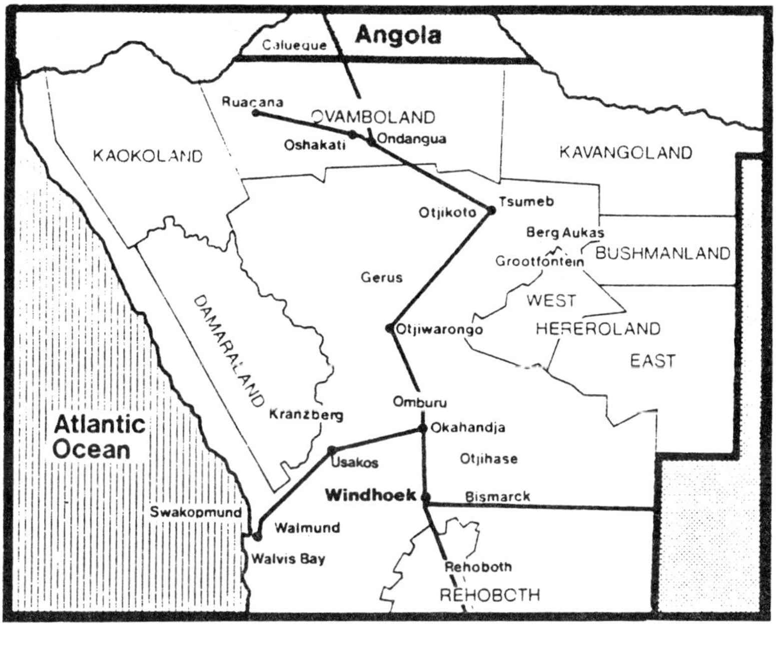

Mikhail Gorbachev must share the same cynical outlook as
Dr. Johnson who, on being told by Boswell that the Corsi-
cans had been in revolt against Genoa for 15 years, expressed surprise that after so lengthy a revolt they should
not have succeeded in tearing down the principal Genoese
garrisons stone by stone "with their bare teeth."

Unlike UNITA in Angola, or the MNR guerrillas in
Mozambique, SWAPO has no permanent bases in Namibia,
cannot claim to control a single kilometer of land, and for
most of the year deploys no more than 40 or 50 men in the
field. Although opinions vary, it is clear that SWAPO does
not pose either an immediate or a major threat to the South
African government. After 20 years its combat strength is
still only 8,500 men, half of what it was in 1978. Not sur-
prisingly, morale is reported to be low. Documents taken
from Jossy Tuutaleni, the information secretary of SWAPO's
Northern Front, during a confrontation with government
forces in September 1985 speak of large numbers of de-
serters and deepening disillusionment at recent reverses.
By comparison there are signs that SWAPO forces in Angola are much better trained and motivated than those operating in Namibia itself. During Operation Askari they appear
to have given a particularly good account of themselves in
the heavy fighting that took place at Ongiva, Cahama, and
Cuvelai.[45]

Even so, this depressing picture hardly bears out the
contention of Lieutenant General George Meiring, the previous commander of the South-West Africa Territory Force,
that the movement is "losing manpower and fighting
soldiers at a rate which cannot be sustained for long."[46]
Depressingly slow progress may have been made, but the
impact of SWAPO's operations has not been without signif-
icance, either in the sphere of politics or defense. Many of
its actions tend to be distorted or never reported; many
incidents that are reported register hardly at all in the international press. Any analysis must make what it can from
the conflicting evidence, most of it partisan, much of it
unreliable. During the first five months of 1985, for exam-

ple, the SADF claimed to have killed 330 out of every 700 guerrillas. It also claimed that in the first eight months of the year, 166 out of the 230 armed contacts had been initiated by the security forces. For its part, SWAPO claimed that its own activities increased threefold compared with 1984, the previous record year.

That the SADF is under increasing pressure, however, seems to be as readily apparent as SWAPO's painfully slow progress. Neither statement is mutually contradictory. Indeed, a number of factors when taken together present the security situation in a rather different light from the official version, one that sits rather uneasily with General Meiring's overoptimistic prognostications.

Since 1984 the number of reported incidents has risen. In 1985, 123 incidents (as opposed to military engagements) were recorded, an increase over 96 the previous year and 41 in 1983.[47] In addition to sabotaging a number of power lines, SWAPO attacked two military bases at Eenhana and Katimo Mulilo as well as the newly completed strategic highway between Oshakati and Ruacana. In October 1985 the local broadcasting corporation reported that all electricity and telephone links between Ovamboland and the Tsumeb mining complex had been severed. The power lines from the Ruacana hydroelectric station were also cut several times during the same period. In short, despite a massive military presence on the Angolan border the SADF was still unable to patrol the area effectively. Nor was it able to defend the economic infrastructure on which the territory relies to attract new investment.

Although the Multiparty Conference in Windhoek is nominally in control of the 27 area force units, 8 full-time battalions, 1 reaction brigade, and the various supporting units that make up the territory's defense force, tens of thousands of South African troops remain entirely outside its control. Because of Pretoria's refusal to establish a defense portfolio for the new administration, it has proved impossible to establish a separate command structure, still less an entirely independent force. In recent years, however,

South African casualties have begun to cause some concern. In some areas, despite recent military successes, the casualty figures have risen sharply. The 101st Battalion stationed at Ondangwa, for example, lost 15 men in the first six months of 1985. Between December 1977, when the unit suffered its first death in battle, and December 1984 only 24 were lost.[48]

Among the white contingents, desertion is on the increase. Of 577 men held in military detention centers in 1981, 519 were serving sentences for refusing to serve in the field or for going absent without leave.[49] Although it is important not to exaggerate the impact of such numbers it would be equally foolish to dismiss them entirely, particularly in a country in which conscript troops constitute the majority of the armed services.

In attempting to evaluate what such statistics may mean in terms of white morale, performance in combat is probably a more telling index of the will to fight than is desertion. Again this is particularly true of a country in which national servicemen see action much earlier than most others. Indeed since October 1981 they have been required to serve for even longer periods in the Operational Area.[50] Between January 1979 and June 1983, 647 national servicemen were killed in accidents and more than 3,000 injured. Only 107 were reported killed in action. These figures seem highly suspect. Either the South African army is unusually accident prone or else casualities in the field have been deliberately disguised as accident statistics.[51]

If this is not the case it is puzzling why the government should have begun to express alarm about the performance of non-regular soldiers. In a private address to the army some years ago, P. W. Botha revealed that only 20 to 30 percent of national servicemen were considered by their commanders to be highly motivated or likely to give a good account of themselves in battle.[52] Whatever the reasons, they are being found disturbingly unreliable under fire. Of the 484 servicemen who were in detention or confined to barracks at the beginning of 1982, 262 were there for refusing to carry out orders.[53] In another report that was leaked to the press in September 1984 and was mentioned by Philip Frankel in his 1984 book on *Pretoria's Praetorians*, conscript troops were accused of deliberately vandalizing military equipment, a problem now so serious that its authors felt justified in using the term sabotage to describe the phenomenon. The report revealed in full the extent of demoralization and disaffection among conscripts, their "poor discipline," and increasing use of drugs. According to another source, a fire that destroyed part of the military base in Walvis Bay, an act that was originally described as accidental by the South African press, was revealed to have been started by disaffected troops. How many such incidents have gone unreported remains unknown.

A further indication that the situation is less reassuring than the authorities claim is the escalating cost of military operations, now running at R1.7 million a day. The cost of killing a single SWAPO insurgent has risen to R600,000, a sum that must prompt one to ask whether South Africa can continue to finance the war on such terms. General Meiring may insist that "figures are not always what they seem."[54] The cost, however, is now so high that it may one day prove as telling as that of the anti-Mau Mau campaign in Kenya when the cost for the British of each insurgent killed passed the £10,000 mark.

As it happens, the cost would be higher still but for the fact that part of the expense has been transfered to the Multiparty Conference administration. Namibia's defense outlays are much higher than the allocation for education (which is not the case for South Africa itself). In 1985 they were double the previous year's figure. The Namibian administration, however, defrays only a fraction of the overall cost of the conflict, no more than R72 million in all. More might be raised but for the fact that local troops are not very effective – their discipline is poor and their black members are demoralized because of meager privileges and inadequate opportunities for promotion.[55]

Finally, the manner in which the war is being fought

suggests intensified not diminished guerrilla activity, which has resulted in ruthless measures to contain it. One sign is that in December 1984, 100 km of the Ovambo homeland along the border with Angola was defoliated, an area extending from Okwayoufuko in the west to Olupale in the east.[56] The disruption to life and livestock must have been considerable.

The defoliation program represents a somewhat crude (and so far ineffective) attempt to create a *cordon sanitaire* along the so-called Yati strip. Recent episodes suggest that those attempts have failed and that the border zone can in no way be compared to the highly effective Morice line, which ran for 400 km from the Mediterranean deep into the Sahara. In the desert conditions that obtained (unlike the lush grassland of Ovamboland) the French found it easy enough to construct three parallel barbed-wire barriers in the 1950s between the frontiers of Tunisia and war-torn Algeria. By comparison, the SADF has been forced to rely on night ambushes at points where infiltration is still possible and on motorized rapid response units that more often than not have managed to intercept infiltrating units before they have penetrated very far. Yet the success rate has not been 100 percent. In January 1983, SWAPO was able to launch a series of incursions into Kavango where, despite crippling losses (up to 900 all told), the movement was able to increase its influence so significantly that two years later it was declared a special security area by the security forces.[57]

Another problem is that the authorities have increasingly relied on elite, highly trained, largely secret special forces who have borne the brunt of front-line operations since 1983. The most well known of the groups is the Buffalo Battalion, which was established in the Kavango Bantustan in 1976 from former members of the Frente Nacional para a Libertacao de Angola (FNLA), one of the defeated movements in the Angolan civil war. Both the 32nd Batallion (as it is officially known) and the Counter-Insurgency Unit (COIN) of the South-West Africa Police are supplemented by two other special units, the South-West African Police Special Task Force and the South-West Africa Specialists, a force directly answerable to the SADF.

Pretoria's reliance on such units is not new, but it is growing, an indication perhaps of its preference for using regular rather than conscript troops and of employing measures with which the regular army might not wish to be directly associated. It would seem that the war has entered a new and more bitter phase, one in which SWAPO may well not prevail by military action. Yet the continuing conflict is also unlikely to secure widespread support for any internal administration the South Africans may set up, which has become the only real justification for their continued military presence.

Finally, perhaps, one of the most interesting comments on the war as well as one of the most depressing was provided by a study of elite opinion conducted in 1982 by Dr. Jan van Wyk. His research revealed that nearly half of the military officers questioned did not believe that, were the territory to be given its independence, South Africa would be "next in line." Yet up to 85 percent of those canvased rejected any idea of negotiating with SWAPO. It is this schizophrenic attitude on the part of the armed forces as well as the government they serve that explains why the war is likely to drag on almost indefinitely, or at least as far as it is useful to speculate.[58]

4

The South African
Defense Industry

They trailed around behind him inspecting the sleek
fighter. "It is called a Mirage. Wonderfully appropriate,"
Lynch said. "It replaces the Sabre which is obsolete.
Not swords into ploughshares you understand? Sabres
into Mirages. . . .
— Christopher Hope, *Kruger's Alp*

There are many ways of measuring military power.
Whatever measurement is used, the armed forces of sub-
Saharan Africa do not appear impressive. Either in terms of
combat, performance, or sophistication of equipment, the
forces of most African states are among the weakest in the
world. South Africa has always been considered the exception because it has a significant industrial base and a substantial, even impressive, domestic arms industry that has
grown up under the stimulus of the arms embargo. Denied
external support, it has been forced to manufacture its own
weapons. ARMSCOR is now the tenth largest arms produc-
er in the world, producing up to 90 percent of the Republic's
needs from heavy artillery to armored vehicles.

It is often forgotten that during World War II South
Africa manufactured a variety of bombs, armored cars, ho-
witzers, antitank guns, and small arms in impressive num-

bers, many years before the first colonial black African state secured independence. Only a reduced market scale and the higher capital investment that was required to produce military goods in the postwar period made it cheaper to import most of its arms in the 1950s, principally from Britain and the United States.

South Africa's armaments industry is now an important part of its economy, one of the largest employers of labor if one includes not only the mainline producers and plants, but also the 400 subcontractors and 1,500 smaller forms involved in the general business of arms production. (See table 1.) Since the production and procurement activities of ARMSCOR were merged in a single operation in 1977, the corporation has gone on to manufacture a wide variety of arms, including the country's first light-attack helicopter, the Alpha XHI, which will eventually replace its obsolescent French and British models. At the annual international airshow in Chile in the spring of 1986, ARMSCOR put on display a wide range of products from the 20-mm GI quick-fire cannon to the first prototype gas turbine engine intended for the country's first unmanned reconnaissance aircraft, the drone.[59]

When one begins to look at the picture more closely, however, it is far less impressive. South Africa may have pilots to fly its planes and technicians to service them, but it does not have an industrial base to sustain a war economy for long. More to the point, perhaps, in peacetime it is still heavily reliant on external assistance, however successfully it may be disguised—a crucial, even potentially crippling, vulnerability for a country threatened with sanctions.

The problem is that South Africa still relies on importing the building blocks of modern weaponry—such as component parts, subassemblies, and other critical technologies. Between 1981–1983 the cost of these imports came to $28 million, more than the total value of the commercial military imports by South Africa over the previous 20 years.[60] Such building blocks are easily assembled. The 155-mm G-5 howitzer, one of ARMSCOR's principal export items,

TABLE 1
Economic Indicators of Arms Production in South Africa

	1968	1972	1976	1980	1984
Armscor turnover in million rand (US $ million at 1979 prices)	32	108 [1971]	(700)	1,500	1,700
Armscor employment (1,000)		12	19	29	(24)
Share of local production in total procurement (%)		30	60	75	80
Share of 'private' sector in local production[a] (%)		50	75	70	60
'Private' sector employment (1,000)			100	90	(80)

Source: Michael Brzoska, Thomas Ohlson, eds., *Arms Production in the Third World* (Stockholm: Stockholm International Peace Research Institute, 1986), 196

[a]'Private' sector includes government-owned companies except Armscor. The figures are official South African figures, the validity of which cannot be checked. They may indicate orders of magnitude only.

which first saw service in Angola during Operation Askari, is modeled on a similar U.S. system. The current type in use in South Africa is powered by a West German motor made by Magirus Deutz; its targeting system uses a computer imported from Canada.

Because a great deal of information is classified, it is difficult to evaluate the extent to which many of ARMS-COR's products are composite models of existing equipment already in use in the West. South Africa's new V-3 air-to-air missile used by its Mirage fighter bombers may well have been manufactured and even designed in the Republic. It is certainly a great improvement on the French Magic system designed and built by Matra. We do not know for certain; we can only surmise.

We are on somewhat firmer ground with some of ARMSCOR's other exports, including the Impala II ground-attack aircraft that was developed originally in 1974 using four airframes supplied by Italy. Even though the South Africans later manufactured the plane themselves, they still relied on Rolls Royce Viper 2 engines built on the insistence of the British government under license from the Italian company, Piaggio.[61] Similarly, although the Atlas Aircraft Company claims that it can manufacture Mirage F-1s from locally made components, a recent study suggests that most of its components are still imported.[62]

South Africa also claims to be able to build lightly armored vehicles such as Eland, Hippo, and Rhino armored cars, some of which have been fitted out with their own version of modern impregnable laminated armor. The Buffel and Ratel models, which were used for the first time in Angola in August and November 1981, both incorporate some genuine innovations, notably the Ratel with its special frontal armor and 99-mile range. Some "locally" manufactured equipment, however, hardly merits the description. The Oliphant tank, for example, is made out of the hull of a British Centurion, probably from the shipment of 1,000 sold by India to Spain for scrap metal, a cargo that surreptitiously found its way to South Africa in 1978 in one of the most embarrassing infringements of the arms embargo.

In the navy, the missile strike craft designated the Minister class are actually Israeli-built Reshefs, three of which were purchased in 1978, the same year as the Centurions. The rest have since been assembled under license in Durban. The Puma helicopter, which forms the backbone of the SAAF's transport helicopter force, is Anglo-French in origin, made up in part of components from Westland, Britain's last remaining helicopter company.

Such evidence suggests that South Africa is much more reliant on foreign licenses and imports than the government is prepared to concede or than some outside observers have recognized.[63] Were South Africa to find itself involved in an extended conflict, there are several reasons to question whether ARMSCOR could either replace the equipment lost or even produce spare parts and components in sufficient quantity. Before looking at this question, however, it is worth discussing South Africa's last remaining link with an external supplier: the government of Israel, on which the future of its next generation aircraft largely depends.

The Israeli Connection

In the 1960s and early 1970s France and Italy supplied South Africa with most of its imported equipment. Together both countries were responsible for 70 percent of all military imports between 1970–1976. Today this is no longer the case. Licensing and coproduction agreements have been terminated; spare parts for earlier sales are no longer in ready supply. Aging frigates have been withdrawn from service; obsolescent European planes have been recycled for spare parts. After 15 years of relentless pressure even the French were persuaded in 1977 to leave the field.

It is clear that if South Africa is a military colossus, it is a colossus with feet of clay. Most of the equipment it purchased from Western Europe has not been replaced. With the Impala line closed down, South Africa urgently needed a new fighter. In July 1986 the air force finally unveiled a modernized jet fighter, the Cheetah, a reconstructed version of the Israeli Kfir. The state has high hopes that with its improved flight control and new integrated weapon and navigation system the plane will be able to meet Angola's MiG-23s on equal terms. It may well be right, but it can only be a matter of time before the Angolans receive even more modern equipment. If the South Africans attempt to engage in an arms race, they will never win. They will never be able to match system for system, plane for plane, only upgrade existing models that are already a generation or more old. Although the SAAF uses NATO nomenclature and operational procedures, it has been left far behind in the past 15 years in force multiplication techniques such as airborne early warning, electronic countermeasures, and smart technology. And although it has recently begun to use cluster bombs, runway penetrators, and retarded or guided bombs, its Mirage F-1As have 50 percent less ordnance delivery capacity than Angola's SU-22s.

For 30 years or more, the defense forces have attempted to replicate the weapon systems of the West, to draw a lesson from Western experience, instead of translating it into South Africa's own needs, determined by its own unique geographical and political imperatives. Were it not for Israeli assistance the Republic might dispose of an aging, low-technology force quite incapable of dealing with some of the future threats it might be called upon to face, even on paper. By 1979 South Africa had become Israel's largest customer with 35 percent of total arms sales.[64] In the future, the Israeli-South African axis (as its critics like to describe the relationship) is likely to revolve around the next generation of light-weight attack aircraft, planes flexible enough for air-to-ground sorties with a backup role as an air interceptor.

South Africa's problems with new generation aircraft are by no means unique. India is an excellent case of a country that has struggled for years to develop a next generation plane, so far without success, despite having one of the largest defense industries in the developing world as well as one of the highest proportions of scientists per capita. Even today it has failed to produce a modern fighter. Its principal attempt, the ill-fated HF-24 Maruta Mach 2, failed in the end because the government was unable to find an appropriate engine or even import one.

It has long been thought that the SAAF has aircraft quite advanced enough for the conditions in which it may have to operate. "Given the relatively simple technology needed for the type of warfare likely to face the South Africans in the near future," Richard Bissell argued in 1982, "it is reasonable to assume that there is more interest in South

Africa in stockpiling weapons to weather some attrition than in moving up technologically."[65] From this premise it was natural to conclude that South Africa would probably become less dependent on foreign imports and less interested in the West as a source of high-technology weapons.

Had the premise been correct the conclusion would probably have been merited. But even at the time the South Africans never shared it. After the fiasco of Operation Savannah, they expressed strong interest in purchasing the Israeli Lavi. Doubtless, they imagined that the United States, although closely identified with the Lavi project, would look the other way if the planes were exported to the Republic, as it had with the Kfir 2, 36 of which have been reputedly purchased by the SAAF.[66] The Lavi actually began life at the conception stage in 1975 when the Kfir program finally came on stream. Long before the Israelis secured U.S. funding for the aircraft there were reports that South Africa might share the costs, a proposal that seems to have been put forward during a secret visit to Pretoria by Israeli Defense Minister Ezer Weizman in March 1980. The following year a rumor circulated, which was never confirmed, that the Lavi might actually be built in the Republic under special license.[67]

In principle, the United States should be able to prevent Israel either from exporting the aircraft or transfering the license. After Weizman's visit, the U.S. Congress committed more than $900 million to the program, a figure which, though large, represented only the cost of research and development. Israel would have needed additional U.S. funds actually to produce the plane—$550 million for 30 planes by one estimate. By the time the project had been completed, the cost might have been as high as $10 billion, a phenomenal sum for so small a country, but one that would have enabled it to deploy the most advanced twin-engine fighter in the Middle East.

In 1986, it was hardly conceivable that it would have allowed South Africa to purchase the plane. But to judge from past experience, neither the Congress nor the Defense Department might have been consulted. Washington might well have been able to prevent the aircraft from being built under license, but it might not have succeeded in stopping the wing and tail being exported as a technology package.

Alternatively, the Israelis could have undertaken minor modifications, thereby claiming it was no longer a U.S. system, as they did with the Sidewinder missile that they subsequently sold to South Africa in the 1970s.[68] If they had installed their own engine rather than the Pratt and Whitney 1120, they might even have claimed that the aircraft was an entirely Israeli system and therefore not subject to outside scrutiny or a veto on reexport.[69] One point seemed beyond dispute. The Israelis would have had to have exported the plane if they were ever to have recovered their development costs, if only because their former Latin American customers had run into payments problems so serious that the Israeli aircraft industry has refused to accept any new orders even at the risk of layoffs in the labor force.[70] If the situation had deteriorated, they would hardly have been able to be overscrupulous about potential buyers.

In any event, the Israelis decided to cancel the Lavi program and to purchase U.S. planes off the shelf. It is by no means certain, however, that cooperation with South Africa will not continue, perhaps on a new version of the Kfir. The link between the two countries still seems very strong.

Defense Industry in Crisis

Where then does South Africa stand? The picture is still confused. In some respects the Republic is clearly in a favorable position. It still has a well-developed industrial base despite the recent recession. The steel industry has been able to develop military steels; it has not been forced to import either barrel or armor steel. Indeed, the development of home-manufactured, laminated armor reveals that vertical integration from the country's mineral deposits to its rolling mills has successfully taken place.

Through its mining industry, one of the most advanced in the world, South Africa has also been able to make a unique contribution to the science of detonics – the understanding of explosives and explosions. It now manufactures 40 propellants and more than 140 different types of ammunition.

Nevertheless, the defense industrial base has deteriorated and is in danger of deteriorating still further, with slow acquisition rates, short production runs, and delayed modernization of the armed services. The high cost of recent military operations has severely reduced ARMSCOR's share of the defense budget, which used to run as high as 70 percent before 1981. (See figure 1.) The collapse of the rand and squeezing of local credit, plus record inflation that has remained in double figures since 1973, has also forced defense contractors to operate at full or near full capacity. In general, the defense industry has been emasculated by low profits and uncertain demand.

It is, perhaps, particularly significant that ARMSCOR has suffered both from high operational costs and reduced defense spending. As a result of this double bind the defense sector in South Africa, unlike the defense industry in the Soviet Union, can hardly be considered "the only true modern sector" in society.[71]

With the increase in SADF operations against the Front Line States, ARMSCOR began cutting back on its 1983–1984 budget. Because of a reduction in real terms in defense spending, coupled with an increase in the activities of the defense force, the corporation had to mark time. Demand for its products fell; in some cases stockpiling ceased altogether. The Impala line was closed down after 239 plants had been constructed (200 assembled domestically). Price limits were also imposed despite defense inflation. As an explanatory memorandum to the 1983 budget reported, "operations are, therefore, increasing at the expense of our capital programme," with the result that the SADF was forced on occasions to use stockpiled equipment.[72]

After the Nkomati accord had been signed some of the capital projects that had been frozen were immediately reactivated. But this time the factories that had been responsible for producing ammunition, shells, and bombs for the operations of 1981–1984 bore the brunt of the second round of cuts. ARMSCOR did its best to offset the losses on one product against the profit margins of others still being built. Where particular products were under pressure and requirements had so fallen that some factories were threatened with closure it tried to offer their products for export at marginal cost, with no contribution to overheads. Many private subcontractors only survived by changing their products altogether.[73]

The problems of adjusting to peace and war reveal just how difficult it is for South Africa to have an arms industry tailored specifically to its own needs. The exact ratio of R & D to profit can only be conjectured. If it is as high as Britain's (2:1) – another power that has opted to build high-technology items that it has often had difficulty selling outside the United States and the Middle East – the only solution would be the road Britain has begun to take in recent years: coproduction (somewhat belatedly, perhaps, because the British still coproduce less than 20 percent of all the weapons they manufacture). Both Brazil and Israel have been mentioned in this context; if either have been involved, South Africa is unlikely to have been the senior partner, lacking the technical expertize or the capital to run programs along lines of its own choice.

Internally, ARMSCOR has made some progress in reducing unit costs by standardizing equipment. The systems management approach, which was introduced some years ago after much opposition, has met with some success. South Africa is unlikely ever again to build the range of armored cars manufactured in the 1970s that often duplicated existing designs – even if the most successful, the Buffel, has now undergone its ninth modification. Finally,

the need to spend within fairly narrowly defined budgetary
limits has forced the corporation to make some difficult
choices, abandoning the idea of replacing the Oliphant tank
or building an entirely indigenous new military aircraft, although it seems to have decided to reconsider replacing its
existing submarine fleet when the present Daphne-class
submarines are eventually decommissioned.

Capacity problems and inadequate financial returns for
private capital prove the point tellingly. The general trend
toward restraint in defense spending makes exports more
vital than ever. Unfortunately, export markets are hard to
find. In the future, ARMSCOR will have to look for markets wherever an opportunity presents itself, as it has in
the Gulf, where G-5 artillery pieces have been sold to Iraq,
and Sri Lanka, where Buffel armored cars have been used to
good effect in the government's anti-Tamil offensive. The
one advantage ARMSCOR has in seeking Third World outlets for its goods is that many of them can be passed off for
what they really are—revamped Kfirs like the Cheetah or
former Centurion tanks. This is not the least of the many
ironies of a deeply ironical situation, one of the many minor
hypocrisies of the international trade in arms.

In marketing its equipment abroad, ARMSCOR has
not been unsuccessful, yet it has found that much of its
best products are either too advanced or not advanced
enough. Why buy from South Africa when one can buy
from Brazil, Czechoslovakia, or Taiwan? If its wares are
often cheaper they are not always what its prospective customers require. Its guns are designed for night firing, its
armored cars to withstand land mines in the parched scrubland of Namibia. Because it has gone for force multiplication many of its weapons need to be downgraded, not up-
graded, for export. Where it has tried to upgrade them
South Africa has frequently found itself without the requi-
site technology.

In addition to these problems, too little money has been
spent on industrial preparedness, with the result that industrial lead times are still quite high. Some manufacturers

have not been able to buy raw materials and components at economic prices. The cutback in government orders and the failure of the SADF to modernize or replace aging equipment in its attempt to keep within the government's spending guidelines have discouraged many defense contractors from introducing new machinery. In anticipation of declining orders some companies have even reduced their capacity. Many raw materials have had to be stockpiled, with consequent high stock levels and reduced turnover figures. Production lines have often been forced to operate well below capacity, but have been kept going to retain industrial skills. Keeping them open has been an expensive undertaking. Capital investment in high technology, high-cost manufacturing plus the cost of testing the equipment, has often been out of all proportion to the turnover figures. Some machines have been used only once a week.[74]

Over the years these problems have become more acute. Many companies cannot afford to specialize in the defense sector despite government orders and subsidized prices. Sandock Austral, which builds Ratel and Eland armored cars, also manufactures turbines for the mining industry, an arrangement that keeps down overhead but also reduces its capacity to start up immediate production. Other companies have been forced to charge inflated prices for the small amount of equipment purchased by the military for current use or stockpiling. At one time, communications equipment cost the army nine times the market price.[75] South African industry still produces diesel engines around one-third more expensive than many imported models. All military vehicles since 1984 have been fitted out with them on the government's instructions.

Among the other problems the defense industry also faces, indeed perhaps one of the most ominous, is its declining capacity to make good not only the loss of hi-tech items such as tactical missiles but also aircraft lost in combat. In 1981, ARMSCOR warned the government that it would be hard-pressed to replace tanks or even armored cars in an extended conflict in Angola. All it could guarantee was the continued supply of small arms and ammunition.[76] At least in the latter sphere its problems are probably at an end. Compared to the 400 rounds for the army's 90-mm cannon that ARMSCOR could produce in 1977, production at its Lenz factory has now risen to 2,000 rounds a day. In terms of local production, South Africa now ranks beside Israel and Taiwan.

South Africa is not so fortunate in the sphere of human skills, many of which are in desperately short supply. Up to 10 percent of the Atlas Aircraft Company's staff has to be recruited from abroad, mostly to work on hi-tech projects.[77] Since 1981 the Mirage force has only been kept going with the assistance of Israeli technicians. If they had not been seconded by the Israeli air force, half the planes would be permanently grounded because of inadequate depot maintenance.[78] In an extended conflict the defense industry may have great difficulty either recruiting people from overseas or negotiating such third-party contracts.

Even if South Africa were to utilize all its engineers and scientists for military purposes, ARMSCOR would still have to recruit abroad. Needing, as it does, 43,000 skilled black white-collar workers a year at a time when less than 3,000 are available, the country simply could not afford to run a Soviet style two-tier economy with preference being given to the defense sector in recruitment of personnel and investment of resources. One of the depressing realities that ARMSCOR faces is that it has been unable to advance black recruits to the level of its white personnel by means of its own apprenticeship and training programs.

Traditionally, the defense industry in South Africa has also been highly labor-intensive. In addition to the problems just noted, many defense contractors have expressed concern that the growth of black trade unions will stimulate demands for increased wages and the continued retention of uncompetitive manning levels. Should either situation come to pass, a serious shortage of indigenous skilled labor would almost certainly arise.

Finally, it is worth asking how South Africa intends to

resolve its quantity/quality quandary. For even if it lowered the quality of its equipment to produce more without relying on foreign components, South Africa could not hope to match the vast amount of arms the Soviet Union has already provided its putative enemies – even war-torn Mozambique, which has received $1 billion of military supplies since independence, including Mi-14 helicopter gunships, PT-76 light tanks, SA-3 missiles, and multiple rocket launchers.[79] Lower quality will not offset higher numbers; it will only reduce performance. The answer, of course, is to increase performance by developing microelectronic technology that would make possible the development of smart weapons. Because costs have fallen so dramatically in the microelectronics industry as a whole, this would also be the most effective way to reduce defense costs.

The trouble is that South Africa relies even for computers on foreign imports; in other hi-tech areas its industrial base is even less developed. Because import substitution would be impossible, South Africa is especially vulnerable to sanctions or disinvestment. Between 1981–1982, for instance, ARMSCOR purchased several Cyber 170/750 computers. Data General also sold a number of MV/8000 computers to a subsidiary of the Council for Scientific and Industrial Research, the defense industry's main scientific body.[80] In the Reagan administration the South Africans were fortunate to find a government that was prepared to disregard its own injunction against selling high-technology defense-related equipment to countries that were not major allies of the United States. This was all the more surprising in the light of the fact that the president of the Council for Scientific and Industrial Research was summoned to Washington to plead his case for the Cyber 170 when it became apparent that Pretoria might soon be able to break the Pentagon's own cryptographic code.

On the other hand, the computer companies are particularly vulnerable to calls for disinvestment. Of the three U.S. companies that dominate the field, two – IBM and Burroughs – have already disinvested. Given such economic and political realities, pressures on Control Data and its competitors to follow suit are almost certain to increase. How long will Pretoria be able to contemplate with confidence a future in which the quality/quantity quandary might count for a great deal more than it does at present? In short, South Africa's defense industry accurately reflects the country's general economic shortcomings. That is why the claim that the defense industry is any stronger than the defense force it sustains is so suspect.

In the end, however, strictly commercial arguments or military analyses are unlikely to carry much weight. ARMSCOR, now the country's largest industrial concern, has become a symbol of South Africa's independence; its production lines represent more vividly than almost anything else the strength of the government's resolve. In private, the country's leaders may entertain doubts about the "total onslaught," but there is political gain in manufacturing weapon systems that will take a decade or more to reach the production cycle. It implies confidence in the state's survival, an implicit belief that its leaders will still be in power in the mid-1990s, besieged and beleaguered though South Africa itself may well be in the interim. ARMSCOR has become a totem, a political fetish for a community that desperately needs to believe in its own future.

5

South Africa and Western Security

Alliance: in international politics the union of two
thieves who have their hands so deeply inserted in each
other's pocket that they cannot separately plunder a
third.

— Ambrose Bierce,
The Enlarged Devil's Dictionary

For many years one of the principal themes of Western
scholarship was South Africa's alleged strategic importance, as well as its alleged contribution to Western security. The South Africans themselves expended very few resources in playing such a role. It required only minor
expenditure on its navy. Even after the appearance of Soviet ships in the Indian Ocean for the first time in 1968,
Pretoria's priorities changed, if at all, only marginally; 80
percent of the defense budget continued to be allocated to
meet a landward threat. Even the main responsibility of the
South African Navy (SAN) remained "to strike inland at
land targets," not out at sea.[81]

Of the three services, the navy has changed most notably in recent years. With the decision by France to suspend
all further arms sales, the SAN was forced to reject many of
the operational concepts of the 1950s. Within a few years

it had become a far more streamlined force, with its sights
set firmly on coastal waters. Antisubmarine corvettes and
expensive frigates gave way to fast patrol boats and inshore
minesweepers. The transformation from a blue-water force
to a coastal unit may have been painful, but by 1980 it was
almost complete.

After 30 years the SAN finally turned its back on a sea
environment that would have required expensive and essentially unuseable ships with their full complement of ship-to-
sea missiles. Once the proud possessor of a squadron of
frigates, the SAN possessed only one, a training ship, not a
fully operational vessel. Even its Daphne-class submarines,
which reached half-life in 1980, were not due to be replaced
once they were finally phased out in the 1990s. Had this
been the case, the SAN would have surrendered its claim to
be the only blue-water navy in sub-Saharan Africa.

A few years ago the navy looked forward to a new class
of locally built submarines and South African corvettes to
replace the remaining two President-class frigates: *President Praetorius* and *President Steyn*.[82] Both were canceled.
As P. W. Botha admitted in his last year as minister of
Defense,

> From now on South Africa's navy will be specially
> geared and designed to coastal defence for protecting
> the sovereignty of home waters. The West will have to
> conduct its own patrols of the shipping lanes to, from
> and around the Cape, and will have to look after its own
> interests.[83]

After 28 years of service even South Africa's naval reconnaissance aircraft — its Shackleton Mark IIIs — were
phased out in November 1984. Hopes of purchasing British
Aerospace 748 Coastguarders came to nothing. South Africa had to rely on its Dakota C-47s to provide a limited
search-and-rescue service — nothing more. Its 27 Albatross-
es based at Cape Town attempted to fill the void, not always
successfully. The Albatross's all-weather radar could identi-

fy large vessels, but not smaller ships; both planes could conduct visual searches only.[84]

Meanwhile the South Africans tried to provide the navy with some over-the-horizon capability by converting a former commercial tanker into a forward-base ship with a flight deck for two helicopters. Unfortunately, the helicopters of the SAAF's No. 22 squadron could carry only a small payload and had a short range.

The contraction of the navy from the ocean-going force of 10 years ago to the coastal force of today was a vivid reminder of the country's diplomatic isolation. The change had a marked impact even on its own regional operations. For there now was no question of South African ships blockading a port in Mozambique or Angola, or mining Namibian waters, or mounting a continuous patrol offshore as the British navy did off Beira throughout the 1960s. The SAN could not even conduct major naval exercises to bring potential enemies into line as the U.S. Navy tried to do in Central America. Such days seemed to have passed for ever.

Because the fear of the Soviet threat is so entrenched in military thinking it is still not clear what influence, if any, the threat of sanctions from the West may have on the security debate. But many are clearly concerned that the SAN has been allowed to run down to a point that can only be described as serious, if not critical. In retrospect, it may seem remarkable that in its threat perception the possibility of a "total onslaught" by the West at some time in the mid-1990s played such a limited role in political thinking; that the Republic's military planners allowed its major surface ships to be retired before replacements were ordered; that the orders for two new Corvettes were not placed until 1976 when the navy's remaining frigates were finally decommissioned; that two Agosta-class boats were not ordered until 1975, five years after the last of the Daphne-class had been delivered; that until recently South Africa only planned to deploy 12 fast strike patrol craft compared with Israel's 23, a country with less than a tenth of South Africa's coastline.[85]

Passing on rapidly from the opportunities that were missed in the past to those that may be grasped in the future, a good case can be made out that the Republic will bse far more vulnerable to Western military action over the medium to long term than a conventional Soviet thrust across its frontiers. The threat of a naval blockade by the West is a far more likely challenge, one involving much less risk for the participants, indeed one that holds out more promise of immediate success given the fact that 91 percent of South Africa's trade with the world is conveyed by sea.

In addition to shipping, particularly the threat to tankers carrying oil, which may be intercepted far off the South African coast at their point of origin or beyond, Pretoria may also have given far too little thought to the possibility of military action against the Kudu natural gas fields off the coast of Namibia (from which it derives diesel fuel) or against the oil platforms that may soon begin to sprout up in Mossel Bay. The government expects these platforms to produce up to 20,000 barrels a day over a period of 15 years during the period of peak production.

The 1977 white paper on defense gave a brief but pertinent summary of the government's understanding of conventional deterrence: "As a counter to the possibility of an attack against the RSA by conventional forces it is considered that a credible deterrent is the best means of discouraging such intention on the part of any potential aggressor." Yet in terms of the potential naval threat posed by the West, South Africa has no deterrent at all, no way of foreclosing the use of neighboring bases such as Diego Suarez or Dar es Salaam from which a naval blockade might easily be mounted, even a minimal "Beira" style patrol of the type which the British navy, using only six ships, mounted throughout the 1960s in an attempt to prevent oil from being transported to Rhodesia.

In the light of their deficiencies it is not altogether surprising that the submarine program, which was abandoned in 1981, has now been reopened in the hope of building a successor to the Daphnes, possibly in collaboration with Taiwan. Blueprints for one of the latest West German submarines have been purchased illicitly, and some West German workers have even gone out to work on their construction. Two old frigates have been brought out of mothballs. The navy is considering buying several new Corvettes from Israel that would be a more suitable replacement for the Type-12 than the canceled Type-69. Earlier in 1986, a new locally designed replenishment vessel, SAS *Drakensberg*, was launched in Durban. Such a vessel would not make sense unless the Corvette program had been authorized as well.

Increasingly anxious to monitor Western naval movements, the South Africans have also negotiated an agreement with Somalia to make use of its ports in return for training members of the Somali air force. (The actual trainers are former Rhodesian air force officers on secondment from the South African government.) They have in addition expanded their presence in the Comoros, where they have an underground monitoring station near Itsandra. As international pressure mounts for sanctions, the establishment of "forward bases" seems to be regarded as vital by South African military intelligence.

It is quite possible that at some point in the mid-1990s the West may be faced with a classic dilemma: either to allow the South African economy to be devastated by sanctions and continued disinvestment or to intervene directly by delivering the *coup de grâce* itself. It is perhaps telling that at the very time that Defense Minister Magnus Malan has strategically downgraded the Soviet threat, a wide range of opinion in South Africa has begun to take the threat from the West increasingly seriously. There now seems to be broad agreement on all sides that the threat to South Africa's security must be defined much more precisely than it has been in the past. What now seems clear is that the total onslaught, far from being abandoned, is merely being recast in a different form — with the West, not the Soviet Union, as South Africa's most immediate adversary.

South Africa and the West

Even if these threats may seem fanciful it is well to recall that there has never been a consensus on security issues between the West and Pretoria, a fact which all the money spent on the Simonstown base was never able to disguise. If South Africa deceived anyone, it deceived only itself. The view from Pretoria was put trenchantly 25 years ago by Professor Jack Spence, although it had first emerged 15 years earlier in the abortive staff talks between Britain and South Africa that followed the signing of the Simonstown agreement in 1955:

> Security is . . . indivisible for the South African gov-
> ernment, not so much in terms of the use to which
> particular weapons systems may be put – but rather
> because of the likelihood that any serious threat to its
> security must of necessity have both an internal and
> external dimension.[86]

The twin elements of internal and external defense seemed to be synonymous because of the belief that Western security interests could not survive the passing of white supremacy. It was not until 1978 that South Africa finally recognized that the West saw "the incumbent government of the RSA only as being incidental to a favourable alignment and not as its cornerstone," to the great puzzlement of Magnus Malan.[87]

Even earlier the West had found its existing links with Pretoria so controversial that it had felt compelled to suspend further arms sales, to cancel the Simonstown agreement, even to reduce to a minimum the use of the Silvermine reconnaissance station, a facility now mostly used by Israel. In 1978 a member of the West German government returned from a visit to South Africa astounded to find how little contact existed even on an informal level between NATO and the South African military.[88] President Jimmy Carter's commissioned studies on the sea-lanes were filed away for discussion at a later date and have never been resurrected. Indeed, South Africa has continued to be strategically downgraded by the Reagan administration in formal NATO deliberations, just as it was under Richard Nixon who chose "to agree to disagree" with the British in 1971 on their decision to resume arms sales to South Africa.[89]

More recently, Western military experts have begun to identify quite a different threat: that of an aggressively neutral South Africa. The South Africans on occasion are clearly not beyond reminding Western governments that it might be inadvisable to push them into "a state of psychic and emotional collapse," a phrase once used by Henry Kissinger in warning the United States not to subject Israel to undue pressure.

As if to confirm these fears, Pretoria introduced strict new controls on the passage of international shipping around the Cape toward the end of the 1970s. It followed up this legislation in 1981 by giving the navy additional authority to stop and search any vessel suspected of carrying arms to guerrilla movements. Occasionally the South Africans have reinforced these measures more directly, by way of reminding the West of its own vulnerability to South African (as opposed to Soviet) interdiction—buzzing a U.S. Carrier Task Force in 1980 as it passed the Cape during a period of particular tension between the two countries.[90] Such incidents may be infrequent, but they serve to illustrate that Pretoria is very much its own master, that it has finally escaped the incubus of the past, that it no longer feels entirely in awe of the West or even responsible to it. As President Botha warned the West in a speech in August 1986, it would be foolish to take freedom of passage around the Cape for granted.

Only Washington's quite unfounded belief that South Africa can still play a role, even a significant one, in the defense of Western security encouraged some strategists to think in terms of an elusive division of labor, even a division of responsibilities. In talks between the Reagan administration and Pretoria in May 1981, the former made known its

desire to achieve "a more positive and reciprocal relationship between the two countries based upon shared strategic
concerns."[91]

The real differences of perception between the two "strategic partners" first emerged in May 1983 after Samora
Machel's decision not to request further Soviet assistance
following a South African attack on Maputo, an action that
first won Mozambique the description of a "responsible"
country in the State Department's political lexicon. In a
secret meeting between the CIA and South Africa's State
Security Council earlier in the year, reported by the *Washington Post*, the Americans had tried without success to
convince the South Africans that their raids into neighboring countries were often ill-timed, especially for those Western powers unfortunate enough to be caught in the slip-
stream.[92] Later that summer the same point was made by
the CIA chief, William Casey, in talks with his South African counterparts in Pretoria.[93]

In the end, of course, the South African view prevailed.
The Nkomati agreement won the argument. Destabilization appeared to have been an unqualified success. Striking
the most optimistic note possible, the U.S. government
greeted Nkomati as a "historical watershed."[94] Vice President George Bush even went so far as to claim that the use
of military power by South Africa could "help establish a
framework for restraint and broad rules of conduct which
[would] discourage the use of outside force in African conflicts."[95] In fact, the Reagan administration's reaction to the
Nkomati process told much more about its view of Soviet
policy in the world than it did about its attitude toward
South Africa. The SADF strategy of destabilization happened to fit into a shared strategic consensus that the Soviet Union was the principal threat, the principal power to be
contained. It followed that as long as the Soviet Union was
forced onto the defensive, its actions would meet with tacit,
often open U.S. approval. This has always been more true of
Angola than it has of Mozambique. In practically his only
pronouncement on Africa during the 1980 electoral campaign, President Reagan informed the *Wall Street Journal*

that if elected, he would provide immediate aid to Savimbi's guerrillas.[96] After the president's failure to persuade Congress to repeal the Clark amendment and Savimbi's own admission in December 1981 that UNITA could not hope to defeat the Angolan government on its own, even if the Cubans withdrew altogether, Washington had only South Africa on whom to rely.[97]

At about this time the SADF began to engage FAPLA's forces directly and in particular to target Soviet-supplied equipment. Much of the 225 million dollars' worth seized in Operation Protea was immediately turned over to Savimbi who was soon able to extend his field of operations as far north as Luanda. Unfortunately, the policy depended for its success on Soviet restraint. For many years the Soviet Union accepted the situation. Far from attempting to carve out a place in the sun, it continued to conduct a highly costly holding operation. Instead of prospecting in the mood of H. G. Wells's Mr. Britling, who had assumed because "everything has become fluid we can redraw the map of the world," Moscow acted with extreme caution.[98] It was precisely because the situation in southern Africa *was* fluid that many of the certainties on which it had acted in 1975 no longer seemed so convincing.

Under Yuri Andropov and Konstantin Chernenko, Soviet policy witnessed what the Russians call a *peredyshka* — a respite, or perhaps more accurately to use Churchill's term, "a loaded pause" — a period of consolidation and risk-avoidance while a country assembles its forces in the wings. With Mikhail Gorbachev's election, the pause has come to an end. The United States, not South Africa, now faces the uphill struggle of maintaining UNITA in the field or watching it melt away into the bush from whence it came.

The Soviet Union, Southern Africa, and Western Security

One of the main reasons the Soviet Union finally decided to act is the change in its perception of the U.S. role in the region, in particular the ambivalent relationship of Washington with Pretoria. Rather reluctantly, the Kremlin seems to have come to the conclusion that the United States is no longer in control of the situation, that far from acting together in accordance with the "new strategic relationship" the two countries had first discussed in 1981, South Africa is no longer a subordinate actor under U.S. direction. It has now become a historical agent, albeit a minor one, in a greater drama of which the United States appears to have no particular understanding.

Since the mid-1970s, one of the most persistent themes of Soviet propaganda was the extent to which South Africa was a U.S. proxy in all but name. Comparing South Africa's intervention in Angola with Israel's in the Lebanon, a Tass statement in January 1984 insisted that both were part of a wider imperialist conspiracy, that neither country would have intervened as decisively as they had "without the support and encouragement of Washington."[99]

Like Israel, South Africa was seen to be a U.S. client that was quite prepared to cross its own version of the Litani River, with or without Washington's connivance. For Moscow the parallels were more than symbolic. In 1984 South African troops staged its exercise, "Iron Fist," in northern Namibia at almost exactly the same time as the Israelis applied the same name to their own operation in Lebanon. Much of what the South Africans did in the region was directly modeled on the Lebanese campaign. Their attack on Maputo in 1983 even tested Israeli publicity techniques used during the siege of Beirut. Pretoria claimed it had carried out a surgical strike against the ANC as had the Israeli government against the Palestine Liberation Organization. The South Africans even employed pilotless planes in the attack, which had been seen for the first time in the Middle East during the 1982 Israeli invasion.[100]

If the two situations differed, the differences were even more ominous than the similarities. For unlike the case of Israel, there were no arms shipments that could be embargoed, no military sanctions that could be applied—perhaps the most telling argument against the claim that the

Reagan administration had succeeded in forging a unique relationship between the two powers. Chester Crocker, the assistant secretary of state for African affairs, might continue to insist that the Soviet Union could be excluded from the peace process in southern Africa as it had been excluded from the Middle East by "building bridges" between South Africa and its neighbors, but Washington's ability to build bridges to Pretoria frequently seemed less impressive than its bridge building to Luanda.[101]

What were the Russians to make of two particularly humiliating episodes involving the United States? The first came in July 1982 when the president's special envoy, General Vernon Walters, assured the Angolan government that there would be no invasion of the country that summer. Hopes were high in Washington that the negotiations over Namibia might at last take off. Yet within an hour of leaving Luanda, the general's promise evaporated as South African troops crossed the border, this time to stay for the next two years.[102] The second episode was even more embarrassing. During talks in Cape Verde in January 1984, Frank Wisner, then deputy assistant secretary of state for African affairs, persuaded the Angolan government not to take advantage of the forthcoming Lusaka accord that was to mark a ceasefire along the border. Far from taking advantage, the Angolans scrupulously honored the agreement. At one time FAPLA forces in the joint monitoring commission found themselves engaged in open battle with SWAPO to bring the movement into line. The South Africans, however, both in their continued support for Savimbi and their delayed withdrawal, flouted the accord from the beginning.

By 1984 it should have been clear that if the differences between Washington and Pretoria were to be found in the sphere of actions rather than aspirations, the United States probably aspired to too much in hoping to use South Africa for its own narrowly defined ends. The Soviet reaction to these events should have been predictable. Anaesthetized for years to the hope that the United States might eventually prevail upon Pretoria to act more responsibly, the Soviet

Union finally woke up to the fact that bridge building (as Crocker understood the term) had not only failed, but that its failure had served to highlight the growing gulf between U.S. aspirations and South African ambitions.

As in Ethiopia and Afghanistan, the new Soviet leadership became more wholehearted in its commitment to the war in Angola, more willing to take risks and even responsibility for the strategy and tactics employed. A dramatic change in the balance of power took place in 1985, with the Soviet Union supplying 23 MiG-23s, 17 MiG-21s, and 10 SU-22s – aircraft particularly suitable for supporting ground attacks. The 25 Mi-25 helicopter gunships it also supplied were ideal for antiguerrilla operations.[103] In addition, Soviet officers began to take part in the actual fighting. In the Angolan government's autumn offensive, 12 Soviet advisers were killed in a single week.[104] It is clear that they not only took part at the brigade and section level, but also that Soviet pilots flew some combat missions.

Soviet relations with Mozambique have always been more equivocal and much less open-ended. In the Andropov and Chernenko years, the sale of military equipment was restricted to a modest number of MiG-21s and Mi-24 helicopter gunships. Despite the visit of a high-level military delegation to Maputo in June 1982, arms deliveries did not increase; indeed, between 1982–1983 their dollar value fell below that of 1978 when relations with South Africa had been more cordial and the threat from the MNR more remote.

Initially, the Soviet Union welcomed the Nkomati agreement as the best outcome to an embarrassing situation. Indeed, Andropov's refusal to provide substantially more military assistance in February 1983 largely forced Machel to conclude the treaty. Far from disciplining Mozambique for coming to terms with Pretoria, the Soviet ambassador, Yuri Seplev, publicly welcomed the agreement and announced immediate further loans. The Soviet Union was even the first international creditor to agree to reschedule Mozambique's debt.[105]

When Nkomati failed, the Soviet Union still looked to

others to bail out Machel, even the United States. But improvement in U.S.-Mozambique relations also began to be thwarted by the U.S. right wing. U.S. aid to Mozambique increased to $66 million in 1985, and in the spring of that year the State Department requested permission that a portion of the funds be spent on nonlethal military equipment – a gesture described by the State Department as a search for "a limited military relationship" between the two countries.[106] Congress turned the request down, and, when the Department requested $1.15 million in nonlethal military aid and training for 1986, Congress made it contingent upon Mozambique's holding elections. Furthermore, Congress restricted development aid to the Mozambican private sector, assistance so limited that the Soviet ambassador was moved to describe the memorandum of understanding more accurately as "a second Nkomati," probably more in sorrow than relief that the first agreement had proved so disappointing.[107]

Since then the Soviet Union has tried to supply Mozambique as best it can. In April 1985 the Pentagon reported that it had delivered at least 44 MiG-21s in the previous 12 months, with recent deliveries far outpacing earlier sales.[108] In September it supplied two Class SO-I patrol boats with a range of 1,000 nautical miles and a speed of 28 knots in the hope of intercepting supplies from the sea to the MNR guerrillas.[109] The impressive Soviet military representation at Samora Machel's funeral in October 1986 signaled to South Africa that it would not tolerate Mozambique's collapse.[110] The failure of the Nkomati process and the demonstrable inability of the South Africans to forge a durable system of regional security finally removed Moscow's excuse for standing on the sidelines of history.

Conclusion

It is clear that there is no real strategic consensus between the West and South Africa, that the Republic is an independent actor, not an ally, a regional power with strictly regional interests operating in a narrow theater of security. All that some U.S. strategists have done is to produce a picture of South Africa's role in the area that is plausible, if at all, only when placed in the wider context of more general strategic ambitions that the South Africans have never shared and that they evince little interest in promoting. At most, Pretoria's forward strategy can be taken only to serve an *a priori* wish to demonstrate that it can play a role in Western security – a phenomenon that social psychologists who have invented the phrase "cognitive dissonance" rather sententiously term "proselytizing after disconfirmation."

To be fair, the South Africans themselves have never made any claim to be willing to subordinate their own interests to those of the West. Indeed, there is no reason why they should. Even after the Nkomati agreement, General Malan insisted on the right to engage in further military operations "regardless of the consequences" even though the United States, as a superpower, might be expected to live with them.[111]

At times, the United States seems totally oblivious to the position that there may well be a threat to Western interests in southern Africa, but that it may not come from the Soviet Union or its Marxist allies. The threat indeed may be more real because Washington is preoccupied by a different challenge altogether – the role of the Soviet Union in the region, a "threat" that seems to justify its exclusion from any role in the management of regional security. Its European allies, by comparison, tend to consider South Africa, a country with which the United States was once "constructively" engaged, a much more irresponsible power.

6

The Will to Resist

The crimes of violence committed for selfish, personal motives are historically insignificant compared `to those committed ad maiorem dei — out of a self-sacrificing devotion to a flag, a leader, a religious faith or a political conviction. Man has always been prepared not only to kill, but to die for good, bad or completely futile causes. And what could be more valid proof of the self-transcending urge than the readiness to die for an ideal. The tragedy of man is not his truculence, but his proneness to delusions.
                                    — Arthur Koestler, *The Ghost in the Machine*

In defending its interests South Africa must ensure that it does not entirely undermine the whites' standard of living, that it does not make enemies of its own citizens. It is this threat that explains why even at this late stage the political landscape in South Africa has not changed significantly. "We already exist in the political, economic, ideological and military circumstances usually associated with a state of war," a SADF commander observed in 1977, the year the government first began referring in public to a "total onslaught."[112] Yet South Africa bears little relation to a society at war, even less to a "garrison state," a description much favored by its critics. For all the much vaunted milita-

rization of South African society there is little prospect of it
turning into a "stratocracy," the term used by the sociologist
Cornelius Castoriadis to describe a totally militarized society in which all resources and priorities are subordinated to
the military sector and the wishes and aspirations of its
defense planners.[113]

Can we really use the phrase garrison state to describe a
country that spends less than 4 percent of its GNP on
defense, a sum considerably smaller than the double digit
percentages of most Warsaw Pact countries? Even by African standards the SADF is not large. Its volunteer element
represents only 3 percent of its total ground forces (active
duty and reserve). As a state, South Africa underspends,
undermobilizes, and underexerts more than many countries
facing lesser threats. Is this situation likely to change in the
near future? Are there any alternatives? Is there any avenue
of escape from South Africa's present security dilemmas?

Spending More for Defense

Much can be learned about a country's determination to
defend itself from the amount that its own citizens are prepared to be taxed in their own defense. On the government's
own admission, that commitment is not as extensive as
many suppose. As Finance Minister Fred du Plessis told
Parliament in introducing his budget in 1985, "the notion
prevalent that defence expenditure is claiming an ever
growing proportion of the budget is simply not true."[114] Military spending for many years has amounted to only 15
percent of state spending, the same figure as 1975, substantially less than in the late 1970s. Not that we should let the
government's own statistics go unchallenged. To judge from
official figures it would appear that recent budget increases
merely represent an attempt to keep pace with inflation. If
we believed that the official figures revealed the whole picture we would be greatly deceived. Take for example the
Special Defense Account, which allows the government to

retain funds for arms required by the services until such arms become available. Its existence largely accounts for the major differences between the regular military budget and total military expenditure. Between 1979–1980 and 1980–1981, the amounts drawn from this account were equal to more than half again the military budget.

Military spending also tends to be hidden away in other departmental accounts. In three out of the last four financial years an additional sum has been made available through the sale of defense bonds.[115] At the moment, millions of rands are being spent on such projects as a new airforce base at Nelspruit and a network of new tactical airfields in the northern Transvaal, paid for from the construction budget. Even the capital expansion of ARMSCOR is being funded by such indirect methods as encouraging private arms manufacturers to sell their products at below market prices in return for nonmilitary industrial subsidies.[116]

And yet, although appearances may be deceptive, although the cash votes for the Ministry of Defense have been exceeded every year since 1981, although the Special Defense Account provided funds equal in value to more than half the annual military budget for the two fiscal years, 1979–1981, although the SADF itself admitted in an explanatory memorandum to the 1983 defense budget that the old cash vote had become "obsolete," there are clearly limits to military spending that the state cannot exceed without alienating its own citizens.[117] The point has probably long been reached where they can be called upon to spend more.

Hidden defense allocations and disguised costs must not be allowed to obscure the fact that defense spending is well below requirement. In 1984 the ministry of defense had to find a larger saving (R150 million) than any other ministry. The following year there were no new major construction programs and no large-scale exercises such as Thunderchariot. Instead there were substantial cutbacks in the defense industry's long-term development programs that will not be felt for some years to come. Even top priority programs such as landward and sea defense, the latter a vast nationwide plan to defend military and industrial installations from sabotage, received only the cost of existing maintenance.

Instead of spending more, the state may well spend less. Cost cutting, not additional expenditure, may be its guiding principle and passion in the relentless battle to reduce the budget deficit still further. Some trends have been noticeable for some time. The size of the SADF may be further cut back in line with the cuts in 9,000 men made in 1984–1985. Unnecessary recruitment may be abandoned; natural wastage may be allowed to take its course. Savings might be made by freezing nonessential capital projects and development programs, limiting border call-ups to a minimum, and reducing fuel consumption on air-training courses. In making the existing budget go much further the government could clearly engage its energies on a front no less broad than that of the SADF itself.

For far too long, of course, the government has balked at making choices, or determining priorities, or even deciding on the exact scope of the defense effort compatible with its overall financial strategy. In short, it has shied away from asking where the Republic's real defense priorities lie, or what kind of defense force it can afford, ignoring the sound principle that the best is often the enemy of the good. Reducing defense expenditure would be a salutary exercise in itself, even though many of the eventual choices might be politically controversial—for example, foregoing the production of such costly systems as long-range artillery and fighter interceptors, the annual costs of which are rising at the astonishing rate of 10 percent a year.

That cuts will have to be made eventually seems inescapable given the high level of state spending in other areas, notably the reform program. Elsewhere in Africa, military spending bears little, if any, relation to political or economic development; in South Africa it is possible to think of it as a social overhead cost. African countries on the whole spend more on defense than they do on social welfare: twice as much on armed forces than on education, six times more than on health. In South Africa the situation differs markedly. Because the total strategy demands "inter-dependent and co-ordinated action in all fields – military, psychological, economic . . . " it follows that military spending can never be given absolute priority, unless and until the state is forced to rely entirely on force to maintain its authority.[118]

The armed forces, after all, are meant to hold the ring against enemies internal and external alike while the government presses ahead with its program of political and economic reforms, with the uphill struggle to narrow the gap between white and non-white incomes.[119] Thus although defense spending increased to a record level in 1983–1984, the increase in education for all races increased even more sharply. Indeed, for the third year running education received more than defense. In fiscal year 1985–1986 the increase in the defense budget was kept down to 8 percent compared with a 19 percent rise for education. Although the defense increase in fiscal year 1986–1987 reached a record 14 percent, the increase in the amount allocated to education was 6 percent higher. In short, just as ghe general increase in defense spending in recent years has arisen from a heightened perception of the military threat, so the impetus for the reform program represents a response to the much more immediate danger of revolution.

The problem is that it is the white voters who have been called upon to find the money for both programs. Their living standards have fallen 20 percent in the past three years as they have been called upon to pay for new schools, new housing, and higher wages for black employees. It is impossible to see, in these circumstances, how the government can expect its own supporters to connive at even higher defense spending without alienating them entirely. If it ever did retreat into the *laager*, how many would follow its lead?

Nonwhite Recruitment

Eighteen years of intermittent warfare on the border have
distorted the SADF structure, producing a dearth of subal-
terns, indeed a chronic shortage of noncommissioned officers. It has also become highly centralized in an age when
centralization is beginning to be equated with inefficiency.
There has been an excessive use of national servicemen in
posts that should be held by career officers and an excessive reliance on conscript soldiers even for normal everyday
combat duties. The case for a larger Permanent Force has
been made quite often, most recently by the former defense
spokesman for the Progressive Federal Party (PFP), Harry
Schwarz, who has argued that it would be "cheaper and
more cost effective in the long run than the effect on our
economy of calling up large numbers of men."[120] Surprising-
ly, the Ministry of Defense has still not undertaken a com-
prehensive cost benefit analysis of the merits of an All-
Volunteer Force (AVF) on the U.S. model.

Although attractive in principle, a regular force would
be far too expensive in practice if public spending is to
remain no higher than 25 percent of the gross domestic
product (GDP). It would require a minimum of six mechanized infantry brigades at a conservative cost of R150
million each, a prohibitively expensive sum when one re-
members that the army would still have to rely on reserves.
If its commanders really are concerned about the morale of
conscript troops, particularly in internal security operations, it might be wiser to promote the creation of a third
force, or paramilitary unit, modeled perhaps on the Italian
carabinieri, a quick response unit as large as the present
police force. Such a force could be drawn from the Citizen
Force or the rural commandos, who might be placed directly under police control. Such a scheme would at least go
some way toward preserving the SADF's much prized "political neutrality," while lessening some of the tensions that
have been highlighted in recent months in joint police-army
operations.

The debate has now shifted to new ground, the benefits to be accrued from having a larger, not a smaller, army that would be capable of undertaking some of the tasks that are beyond the SADF as it is currently constituted. The obvious solution would be to relieve the pressure on the white community by extending the recruitment of nonwhite soldiers, to pursue what the defense white paper of 1973 described as "a more equitable division of the defence load among all population groups." Among the chief findings of the recent government committee chaired by General Geldenhuys was that while national service should remain, volunteers should be sought among all population groups. The most likely of the groups is the Coloured population. The South African Cape Corps was the first nonwhite unit ever to be commissioned. The 2nd Cape Corps Battalion took in its first draft of trainees in January 1986, effectively doubling the intake of Coloured infantrymen. The problem for the government threatens to arise not from the absence of volunteers but from any decision to extend conscription.

Since the early 1960s the state has targeted the Coloured community for future military service, although it has never admitted as much, introducing cadet forces in the schools, and running outdoor "adventure" courses for the young. It also set up a paramilitary training scheme in the Western Cape, which was abandoned only after thousands of youths refused to register and many others fled from the camp.

The 1986 white paper in the end reiterated Malan's undertaking that there would be no conscription of Coloureds and Indians without the agreement of the House of Representatives and the House of Delegates, two of the parliaments in the new tricameral constitution. Because the delegates in both have only been elected on a 20 percent turnout of the population, the government could hardly expect to win general acquiescence, let alone support, for conscription on the grounds that two of the three nonwhite communities now have the vote.

Yet one of the principal tests of the new constitution

will sooner or later have to be whether the elected members
of the two legislatures in their role as nonportfolio members
of the cabinet are allowed to sit in the State Security Council (the body in which military decisions are largely taken).
As the American academic John Seiler and his South African colleague Deon Geldenhuys have persuasively argued,
will they be able to acquiesce in their own exclusion much
longer without forfeiting even more popular support? If
they were elected would the army ever trust them with
highly sensitive information, given that Alan Hendrickse,
whose Labour Party won the majority of seats in the Coloured parliament was actually detained by the security services in 1976? If they were not to be entrusted with such
information would they ever be able to endorse further military raids against the FLS or the future use of the army to
restore order in the black townships?[121]

More problematic still, if they ever did go along with
such decisions how long would they retain the confidence of
their own communities? As events stood at the end of 1986,
few of them could view the prospect of contesting the next
election without acute concern. There is a distinct possibility of the dismally low polls of 1984 slumping still further at
the next election. This is what happened in the case of the
Coloured Persons Representative Council when the number
of voters participating in the election of 1975 was between
30 to 40 percent lower than in 1969.

The recruitment of blacks presents an even more
thorny problem. Black recruits still represent only 12 percent of the full-time force compared with 13 percent for
other nonwhite contingents.[122] In principle, there is no real
reason why more blacks should not be recruited especially
during a period of record unemployment. During World War
II, black soldiers formed 37 percent of the SADF. In practice, however, even voluntary recruitment has proved a sensitive issue. Even if more volunteers did join up it is unlikely that their induction would be as rapid as that of the
Coloureds and Indians, whose numbers increased by more
than 40 percent between 1977–1978, in a single year.[123]

Tensions within existing black units (all but one of them divided on a tribal basis) are already something of a problem. A number of recent cases have been reported of troops deserting, selling their weapons, or even refusing to carry out orders. These incidents may increase in frequency if service morale is further undermined by an ANC campaign that has sought to make clear that "there is no place in our communities for those who wear the uniform of apartheid and carry out orders to kill, maim and torture their brothers and sisters," the grim warning issued by the movement's national executive committee.

Experience elsewhere in Africa during the colonial period suggests that on the whole most volunteers, whatever their race or creed, tend to remain loyal to their commanding officers and, by definition, to the state, that the professional ethos often exerts a greater pull than nationalist sentiment. But the situation in South Africa could prove very different, as it has in so many other respects, if the moral pressure on black recruits were to escalate still further. During the Soweto uprising the families of the 21st Battalion had to be evacuated for fear of their personal safety. Similar concern was expressed during the riots in the Cape in 1985–1986 in the course of which 550 policemen and their families had to be relocated to white areas. If these circumstances were to be repeated on an even more extensive scale it is difficult to see how service morale would not be affected adversely.

As for the issue of conscription, neither the experience of Rhodesia nor Namibia is reassuring. By the end of the Rhodesian struggle 50 percent of the security forces were black. Voluntary service proved highly successful; conscription did not. Introduced at the very end of the conflict in September 1978 it met with widespread resistance and resentment. Of the first 1,554 blacks who were notified for the January 1979 call-up only 250 reported for duty, and among these desertions were almost an everyday occurrence. Significantly, university entrance, which made black students automatically eligible for military service, dropped dramatically. The incoming class of 1979 was the smallest in the country's history. Subsequent intakes between March and September were poorly subscribed.[124] Presumably Pretoria would wish to recruit from university entrants for ranks up to and beyond that of major; indeed, it would need to do so in its search for a black middle class, a citizen force reconciled if not to the prevailing political order, at least to "joint survival," to a system of orderly rather than revolutionary change.[125]

In Namibia the government has already introduced universal conscription for all males between the ages of 18 to 55. Sixty percent of the South-West Africa Territory Force (SWATF) is indigenous; of this percentage three-quarters are black. One of the tragedies of the present conflict is that blacks are now fighting against each other. Many have been forced to join the security forces for employment — very few out of conviction, most simply to get paid. With the economy in ruins and unemployment spiraling out of control, white factory owners and farmers have been able to present their workers with the choice of leaving the country to join the 100,000 already in exile, or entering the army for two years or longer. With few pleas for deferment or exemption allowed, the workers have little choice but conscription or loss of their jobs.

Nevertheless, opposition to national service is already beginning to mount. The South-West Africa Union, the Independence Party, the Christian Democratic Party, even the Damara Council, which represents the territory's second largest tribal group, have all voiced their opposition to recruitment by an "occupying" power. More vocal still has been the Namibian Council of Churches, which has repeatedly warned that South Africa's present policy is pushing the country closer to the brink of civil war. For that reason it is hard to imagine any major movement in South Africa endorsing national service or even lending its support to the future recruitment of volunteers. They would be bound to see it as a transparent attempt by the government to engage in the age-old policy of divide and rule.

This, of course, is precisely its rationale in Namibia. As Lieutenant General Meiring admitted with disarming candor, he saw no problems integrating a postindependence SWATF with SWAPO guerrillas "because a post-independence government will not be Marxist and therefore will not accept SWAPO terrorists into the ranks."[126] Far from trying to create a body above tribalism, a truly Namibian force, Pretoria has pressed ahead with creating two tribal units in the Owambo and Kavango homelands (Etango and Evunza), which though too small to make a major political impact may well become a quasi-military tribal opposition force to the current SWAPO leadership.

If the present tribal units in the SADF are pushed into fighting on the border areas while white troops are held back and if the NCOs come to regard themselves as a professional cadre within the state they too may aspire to the rank of an elite, regarding the avowedly nontribal ANC with increasing suspicion. For that to happen, the terms and conditions of employment for blacks would have to improve considerably. It is true that the military disciplinary code was amended in 1975 to give black officers the same status as whites of equal rank. In the intervening years, however, the rule has been effectively circumvented by the current practice of recruiting from the ranks rather than from the universities and for establishing tribal units especially in the northern Transvaal where the emphasis has been on building up black combat auxiliaries in the rural commandos. If segregated units and differential treatment continue to discourage bright university and nonuniversity graduates from pursuing a military career, it would be surprising if more black officers did not turn to nationalism. If individual units perform well in the field, this will not necessarily vindicate present policy but merely bear testimony to the character and training of the individual soldier.

Conversely, the speeding up of black recruitment could rid Africanization of many of its present invidious features. If military expediency were to dictate policy, the black intake would inevitably rise. This might well be a progressive

idea, perhaps even a necessary one, if the racial divide is to
be bridged. So far, however, it has lacked imagination and at
worst still smacks of institutionalized racism. The government's present failure to recruit more officers from among
the nonwhite units must cast doubt on its new found faith
in the "one nation" idea. So far the history of black recruitment has been one of wasted opportunities and disappoint-
ed hopes.[127]

The Nuclear Option

If the SADF does not find more money to spend and if
black recruitment continues to hold out little promise, there
may well be a passing temptation to look at the escape
route the Western powers have taken to reduce the need for
ever spiraling defense expenditure: nuclear deterrence. As
Deputy Defense Minister Kobie Coetsee remarked in September 1980

> As a country with a nuclear capability it would be very
> stupid not to use it if nuclear weapons were needed as
> the last resort. . . . [128]

As the years pass there may well be increasing talk of a
nuclear option. The threat is not of nuclear warfare as such.
Significantly, for a country like the United States with a
vigorous antinuclear movement and a vociferous antiapart-
heid lobby there has been no perceptible reaction to Bishop
Desmond Tutu's warning that a desperate white government might be quite capable of using nuclear weapons at
the eleventh hour.[129]

There is no real prospect of a nuclear exchange between
South Africa and its neighbors or even a low-yield nuclear
conflict in the bush. Presumably, however, the Republic
might consider using tactical nuclear weapons against specific troop embarkation points if faced with an actual invasion. If South Africa actually possessed nuclear weapons
such a contingency, although remote, could not be ruled

out, especially if the security forces found themselves engaged on two fronts simultaneously — facing industrial and urban violence at home and a conventional war on the frontier.

It has been generally assumed for some time that South Africa has the potential to manufacture nuclear weapons, either by following the plutonium or uranium routes. The main limitation on the former is that its Pelindaba reactor and Koeberg plant are governed by the rules of the International Atomic Energy Association (IAEA), not to mention bilateral agreements entered into with the United States and France. The uranium route seems the more promising. Indeed, one expert suggested some years ago that Pretoria would have been able to have produced sufficient material from its unique uranium enrichment process for at least one bomb by August 1977 and possibly as many as eight by the end of 1980.[130]

In 1979 the Carter administration had to deal with more concrete evidence: the possibility of an Israeli-South African nuclear test in the southern Indian Ocean. Six years later, Representative John Conyers released 500 pages of technical documents obtained under the Freedom of Information Act that appeared to confirm what many people had suspected at the time: that Washington had "summarily dismissed" the initial evidence of the test — a recording by a Vela satellite that had been specifically launched to monitor all such nuclear tests, together with other corroborative evidence. In his report Conyers claims that the White House refused to accept the findings of a naval laboratory, the Defense Intelligence Agency, and the Los Alamos National Laboratory on the grounds that their collective evidence was "inconclusive."[131]

Whether the 1979 incident took place or not there does seem to be *prima facie* evidence of an Israeli interest. It seems clear that the Israelis have had the capability to explode a 2–4 kiloton device for some time.[132] They have also shared civil nuclear technology with South Africa since the 1960s. When Israeli scientists developed a laser method of uranium enrichment in 1970, South Africa, with its own uranium enrichment program, must have immediately suggested itself as a suitable partner. Together with its uranium reserves and a vast coastline suitable for carrying out nuclear tests, such a partnership would be exceptional, but not surprising.[133] If the Carnegie Endowment for International Peace is right in its study that South Africa acquired nuclear weapons in 1980, the Israeli link would seem the most likely.[134]

Certainly, it is in South Africa's interest to let its enemies think it has a nuclear capability. In 1985 the government allowed Agence France-Presse to publish a claim by a former South African diplomat attached to the IAEA that it was now capable of building at least two nuclear bombs a year.[135] Some experts believe that even its new G-5 cannon is capable of firing nuclear projectiles. In addition, reports that Israel has deployed 20 Jericho-2 nuclear missiles in the Negev desert suggest that South Africa's own Jericho missiles would be a suitable delivery vehicle for more lethal weapons.[136] Presumably either system could be used to preempt an impending attack or break up a concentration of conventional forces, an option that would involve little collateral damage to the civilian population in the sparsely populated scrubland of the Western Cape or the flat desert country of Namibia.

The only problem with the nuclear option, as the United States discovered in Korea and Vietnam, is that deterrence tends to break down when the opposing side does not possess nuclear weapons. For a pariah state like South Africa to cut a nuclear figure in a world of non-nuclear states might be exceptionally unwise. With the single exception of Nigeria no African state has yet ever spoken of deploying nuclear weapons or allowing them to be deployed anywhere on the continent. Most of them are sensible enough to recognize the value of what Professor Denis Austin in a felicitous phrase once called "the security of impotence."

Possession of the bomb could end any remaining hope South Africa might have of using force in the struggle for majority rule, quite apart from the immediate danger it might run in engaging in nuclear politics. If two opponents as ideologically opposed as the Soviet Union and the United States have been forced to coexist because of nuclear weapons, is it impossible to imagine South Africa and its neighbors being compelled to connive at the continuing existence of the other? If, as Nikita Khrushchev once claimed, the bomb cannot recognize "the class principle," it is hardly likely to distinguish between races. To quote the English historian John Morley, history may never stop short, governments invariably do. Unfortunately, most African states find themselves in no position to make history at all.

Retreating into the *Laager*

Were South Africa ever to feel really threatened, many of the constraints that we have just discussed might soon disappear. More money could undoubtedly be found; black recruitment might be pursued with a breathless disregard for the consequences; even the development of nuclear weapons might provide a much needed moral boost. It is always possible that the garrison state could become a reality. So far the government has shown no interest in this option. It has tried to play down the scale of the township violence, the extent of the war in Namibia, even its own raids into neighboring states, largely for fear of international reaction. This was both unexpected in its virulence and scope after the introduction of the first state of emergency in 25 years.

The need to avoid policies that might forfeit what remains of international support already seems to be of much greater importance than the adoption of measures that, in principle, might be capable of containing, if not reversing, the violence. The decision to increase the size of the police force not the army, the prolonged hedging over martial law, which was introduced in only 35 districts not the 120 in 1960, even its early rescinding, betrayed a reluctance to rely on force or to press matters to a conclusion. The first state of emergency affected only 2 percent of the Republic's total surface area. Now that the state of emergency has been reintroduced it will probably remain in force for a good deal longer. What is interesting, in retrospect, is the government's over-measured response in 1985 compared with its relentless and ruthless repression in the three years after Sharpeville.

Even if sanctions are applied and South Africa is forced into greater isolation, the government may continue to underestimate the strength and extent of black opposition, to deceive itself that it can probably be broken without recourse to more ruthless measures, to hope – despite all the evidence – that the ANC will be neither determined nor resilient enough to make tougher measures necessary. Force if used may lack direction. The government may go on deluding itself that the majority of blacks are not hostile to reform, merely "terrorized by the ANC." There may be no real attempt to assess the strength or existence of the silent majority on which the entire policy of reform, of *not* retreating into the *laager*, largely turns.

The need to react to the violence without alienating the moderates or abandoning the reform program will be a formidable undertaking, a difficulty encountered by all governments attempting to grasp the nettle of dealing with political revolt without alienating the entire population. In the case of South Africa the authorities will probably be no more successful than the British were in Ireland in the early 1920s. The task may well be beyond any government, however imaginative. The belief that it *is* possible, however, may well sustain Pretoria in its determination to remain outside the *laager*.

The army itself is unlikely to force the issue. The military are likely to be as much a party to this self-deception as the politicians. In recent years the military intelligence staff has become so inward looking that it has vainly cultivated political constituencies that either do not exist or have little following. It is not in the nature of armies, of course, in any but the most democratic societies, to stand on the sidelines as the state collapses around them. Indeed, they cannot afford to because in politics the habitual avoidance of risk is often the beginning of the irremediable collapse of the will. But the armed forces in South Africa are still Pretorians, not a Praetorian guard with political ambitions of its own. Although there has been much talk of a military coup, the army is desperately trying to remain politically neutral. As long ago as 1977, Magnus Malan expressed concern about "the problem of reconciling democratic principles with the total strategy."[137] That concern is still real.

To that extent, the armed forces remain wedded to the political principles of a different era, lacking the breadth of vision to break with a past that can no longer serve as a reliable guide to the future. At the moment of crisis the generals have not been able to divest themselves of the memories of the 1960s and to acknowledge that the total strategy is obsolete, that South Africa can no longer afford to invest in a defense industry geared to a long and bitter struggle against an external rather than internal foe.[138] Having long been a leading exponent of the reform program, the army seems to have lost the essential ingredient for survival: a willingness to change itself.

On strictly military grounds, of course, the army is probably quite right to eschew a more ruthless approach. Although a number of commanders are strongly sympathetic to the view that it *is* possible to control the urban population, the French experience in Algeria suggests it is not. General Jacques Massu may have been given absolute freedom of action to clear the Algerian nationalists out of Algiers in January 1957, the only time the French ever fought the nationalists with their own weapons – terror and torture. Massu's methods, however, eventually proved counterproductive. He succeeded, but at an unacceptable cost in a campaign in which more than 3,000 people disappeared and in which the French political system was strained almost to the breaking point. By freeing army units from political control, the politicians also encouraged the growth of private armies whose commanders' first loyalty was to their own men, not the state.

Clearing the townships of radical elements might still be possible, but the political consequences would be disastrous. In the first instance, the country would invite sanctions on a scale that the Fourth Republic never had to fear or face; in the second, a military solution would be possible only by pressing military action to its limits along a well-defined course that had unequivocal public support. Clearly, many senior officers already believe that the government forfeited any chance of such support when it sent conscript troops into the townships in the summer of 1985 and that it could certainly not rely on it if it ever chose to transform South Africa into a garrison state. The military is concerned that the political situation in South Africa might well get out of hand, but the advice it has given the government has been essentially political: to speed up the pace of reform while simultaneously foreclosing the ANC from making contact with an ever-widening section of the population by restricting the free flow of ideas and information that has always been one of the few civil liberties the state has permitted.

In recent years the Defense Staff College has focused its attention away from the threat of Marxism to that of black nationalism in belated recognition that the ANC's appeal lies not in its policies (which it has been reluctant to outline), but in its broad-based support within the country from the "young comrades" in the townships for the United Democratic Front (UDF). The experience of the township riots has made the army no more confident than before that there can ever be a purely military solution to South Africa's problems, but it has made it far less willing to tolerate a judiciary that has allowed trade unionists to escape prosecution for membership of the ANC or tolerate a press that has won the right to print the names of political detainees. Over the next few years the Republic will probably discard what remains of the system of government inherited from the British. That will in no way imply, however, that it will become a garrison state, only a more ruthless, possibly a more effective, one in defense of whatever political dispensation it may decide to summon into existence, however fictional or real.

In the future, the government and the army will have history firmly in mind. Their actions have been governed by past events as well as present experience. From past history there has come an advanced state of wariness and, particularly, distrust of the West; current experience has made them even more cautious. Both may make them more intractable. It remains to be seen whether political isolation will hail them within range of the certainties of the past or the uncertainties of the future.

If the former, the West may at least be able to draw one crumb of comfort in an otherwise depressing political vista. If history is still a potent force in Afrikaner politics, we should always remember that it teaches one important lesson. It is often forgotten that the *laager* was an offensive not a defensive device, a means by which the Afrikaners were able to regroup in their long trek into the interior during the years of expansion in the latter half of the nineteenth century, a period when they defeated Xhosa and Briton alike, when in the 1880s they mounted the first successful nationalist revolt against colonial rule. As a defensive instrument the *laager* may have served Andries Pretorius especially well at Blood River in 1838, but in defense it served General Piet Cronjé particularly badly at the battle of Paaderkraal in 1900. Of the many options open to the state in its final tryst with destiny, retreating into the *laager* may be the least compelling of all.

Conclusion

If the government were to change the way it looks at defense, many of its present problems might, of course, be avoided. To begin with, the *laager* offers no escape from the future; even if the country's present defense policies offer little hope of escaping from the past. The best course the SADF could follow is to take to heart two valuable lessons contained in the British writer Paul Johnson's *History of the Modern World*. The first is that the best that any status quo power can hope for is stability, however imperfect: "To promote dynamism is to invite chaos." Moreover, because such powers are frequently forced into painful retreats from carefully prepared positions, stability is most likely to be achieved by "selecting those positions which must be defended and (can) only be defended by force, . . . devising workable alternatives for the others."[139]

As South Africa awaits the end of white supremacy, both lessons seem to be particularly relevant. The very dynamic of forging a *Pax Pretoriana* has hardly been in the state's real interests, however successfully it may have conveyed to the outside world an illusion of power. The attacks on neighboring countries have been an unquestionable dynamic, but they have been unfortunate in their consequences. Faced with the severing of its communications links, the ANC has been forced to switch tactics in a manner that has transformed it from a somewhat obscure liberation movement (disorganized and demoralized by its expulsion from Mozambique) to the status of a potential government in exile.

In addition, by highlighting the West's reluctance to intervene, as well as the Soviet Union's inability to defend its own allies in the region, the SADF's very success has merely confirmed South Africa's black population in an opinion they have long held: that little, if any, significant external support can be relied upon or expected in the conflict that lies ahead. As the leader of the United Democratic Front told its members after the signing of the Nkomati accord, "The first thing you will have to do is to forget that others will liberate you. If you want freedom you will have to fight for it yourself."[140] After the West's failure to respond to South Africa's first attack on Maputo in February 1981, even Mangosuthu G. Buthelezi, the most moderate of the black political leaders, conveyed much the same message to his own supporters.[141] It was a lesson that the young militants in the townships took very much to heart in the winter of 1985.

There is no reason to believe that the present military leadership in South Africa will make any headway where the previous generation has failed; but even to make the attempt they would need to rid themselves of the myths that have long obscured a true understanding of the country's security dilemmas. One of the most compelling is that any successful policy must be dynamic. A second is that it must be expensive.

On the contrary, there is no reason why South Africa should not return to a more minimalist defense posture; an all-volunteer force, leaner but better trained; a less wasteful defense industry more appropriate for the country's needs. In fact, there is no reason why the government should not return to the priorities outlined in the 1962 white paper on defense. These priorities were set in the days when the armed forces were expected to do no more than maintain order at home rather than engage in ambitious campaigns beyond the frontier, or plan for a total onslaught that from the earliest days of its conception has always seemed more hypothetical than real.

There is no evidence, of course, that the government intends moving in that direction. Instead, the depressing reality of South African politics is that neither the politicians nor the generals have made any real attempt to define the limits of military power. Furthermore, they have not defined the state's genuinely defensible positions, even though the imposition of sanctions makes the exercise more urgent than ever.

Notes

1. Richard Booth, *The armed forces of African states*, Adelphi Paper 67 (London: International Institute for Strategic Studies, 1970), 2.

2. Chester Crocker, "Current and Projected Military Balances in Southern Africa," in Chester Crocker and Richard Bissell, eds., *South Africa in the 1980s* (Boulder, Colo.: Westview Press, 1979), 71.

3. L. H. Gann and Peter Duignan, *Why South Africa Will Service* (London: Croom Helm, 1979), 202.

4. Gann and Duignan, 241, f. 16.

5. Jacques Ellul, *De la revolution aux revoltes* (Paris, 1972).

6. Diana Russell, *Rebellion, Revolution and Armed Force* (New York, N.Y.: Academia Press, 1964), 53–54.

7. *Financial Mail*, March 15, 1985.

8. Estimates compiled by the Institute of Strategic Studies, Pretoria, *Weekly Mail*, November 15, 1985.

9. *Star* (Johannesburg), August 12, 1986.

10. Cited in Heribert Adam and Hermann Giliomee, *Ethnic Power Mobilized: Can South Africa Change?* (New Haven, Conn.: Yale University Press, 1979), 253.

11. *South Africa Digest*, August 28, 1981.

12. For a police view of "minimum force" see Major General A. J. Wandrag, deputy commissioner, South African Police (riot control): "The police have learnt from experience, as was the case during the 1976 Soweto riots, that the concept 'minimum force'

also implies that bloodshed and violence can in the long run only be limited to the minimum if the situation is nipped in the bud by firm police action in the initial stages." "The Police and Political Unrest," *Strategic Review* (Pretoria) (October 1985).

13. *South Africa Report*, January 18, 1985.

14. *Cape Times*, April 5, 1985.

15. Colin Legum, ed., *Africa Contemporary Record 1981–2* (New York, N.Y.: Africana Publishing Co., 1983), B764.

16. Kenneth Grundy, "Bearing the Burden of War: When the People Pay the Piper but Seldom Call the Tune" in Olijake Oluko, ed, *Southern Africa in the 1980s* (London: Allen and Unwin, 1985), 215.

17. Gann and Duignan, 213.

18. *White Paper on Defence and Armaments Supply 1973* (Pretoria: Department of Defense, 1973), 1.

19. Mathias Hougen, parliamentary commissioner for the Reichswehr, cited in the *Economist*, March 14, 1970.

20. *Guardian*, May 21, 1983.

21. Richard Leonard, *South Africa at War: White Power and the Crisis in Southern Africa* (New York, N.Y.: Lawrence Hill and Co., 1983), 16.

22. Merle Lipton, *Capitalism and Apartheid* (London: Temple Smith, 1985), 109.

23. V. S. Naipaul, "Conrad's Darkness" in *The Return of Eva Peron* (London: Penguin, 1980), 184.

24. *Africa Confidential* 25, no. 21 (October 17, 1983), 5.

25. Cited in Kenneth Grundy, *The Militarisation of Southern African Politics* (London: Tauris and Co., 1986), 74.

26. *Drum 6*, no. 4 (1982): 11–14.

27. The quotation comes from J. M. Coetzee, *Waiting for the Barbarians* (London: Penguin, 1980). "Empire has created the time of history. Empire has located its existence not in the smooth recurrent time of the cycle of the seasons, but in the jagged time of rise and fall, of beginning and end, of catastrophe."

28. Operation Thunder Chariot "involved 11,000 troops in a conventional set-piece battle. The exercise threw tanks and heavy artillery into an assault on 'enemy' positions in the northern Cape region ... Robert Jaster, "South Africa and its Neighbours," Adelphi Paper 209 (London: International Institute for Strategic Studies, 1986), 19.

29. Lombard, "South Africa: The Economic Aspects of Na-

tional Security, Some Policy Considerations," in M. H. Louw, *National Security: A Modern Approach* (Pretoria: Institute of Strategic Studies, 1978), 84–99.

30. Leonard, *South Africa at War*, 102.

31. For the first concept see Colin Legum, ed., *Africa Contemporary Record 1977-8* (London: Rex Collings, 1979), B916. *Defence White Paper 1977* cited Thomas Henriksen, "Namibia: A Comparison with Anti-Portuguese Insurgency," *The Round Table* (April 1980), 189.

32. *Times* (London), September 18, 1985.

33. Barry Buzan, *People, State and Fear: the National Security Problem in International Relations* (Brighton: Wheatsheaf Books, 1983), 65–73.

34. Kenneth Grundy, *Confrontation and Accommodation in Southern Africa* (Berkeley, Calif.: University of California Press, 1973), 71.

35. *Sunday Times* (London), September 15, 1985.

36. *Africa Now*, March 1984, 22.

37. *Times* (London), October 3, 1985.

38. *Observer* (London), October 20, 1985.

39. Cited in Colin Legum, ed., "The Continuing Crisis in Southern Africa" in Legum, ed., *Africa Contemporary Record 1983-4* (New York, N.Y.: Africana Publishing Co., 1985), A45.

40. *Sunday Times* (Johannesburg), October 27, 1985.

41. *Citizen*, August 30, 1985.

42. Ibid.

43. *Guardian*, March 15, 1985.

44. *Times* (London), March 16, 1985.

45. *Economist*, March 30, 1983.

46. "The Terrorist War against South-West Africa," *Southern Africa Facts Sheet*, No. 80 (February 1986), 6.

47. *Africa Economic Digest*, January 4, 1986, p. 16.

48. *Sunday Tribune*, September 22, 1985.

49. John Reed, "Front Line: South-West Africa," *Armed Forces*, February 1984, p. 60.

50. *Guardian*, October 16, 1981.

51. Philip Frankel, *Pretoria's Praetorians: Civil-Military Relations in South Africa* (Cambridge: Cambridge University Press, 1984), 138.

52. Ibid., 137.

53. *Observer* (London), September 9, 1984.

54. *Sunday Tribune*, September 22, 1985.

55. *FOCUS* 61 (November/December 1985), 11.

56. *FOCUS,* 57 (March/April 1985), 9.

57. For one of the best summaries of the bush war see André du Pisani, "SWA/Namibia Update 1981 to April 1984," *Africa Insight,* March 14, 1984. Since that report was compiled, it is only fair to point out that SWAPO seems to have met with much less progress even in Ovamboland and that its casualty rates have risen dramatically.

58. J. J. van Wyk, "Elite Opinions on South African Foreign Policy," *Research Project on South Africa's Foreign Relations, Occasional Paper No. 1* (1984), 25–29.

59. *South Africa Digest,* March 21, 1986.

60. *Star,* January 16, 1984.

61. *Southern Africa: The Escalation of a Conflict* (Stockholm: Stockholm International Peace Research Institute (SIPRI), 1976), 139.

62. *South Africa: Time Running Out,* Study Commission on US Policy Toward Southern Africa (Berkeley, Calif.: Berkeley University Press, 1981), 251.

63. See, for example, Chester Crocker's claim that with the delivery of 1,000 Centurions in 1978, together with South Africa's ability to recondition their engines and replace their guns, South Africa could no longer be considered dependent on the international arms market. Chester Crocker, *South Africa's Defence Posture: Coping with Vulnerability,* Washington Paper, no. 84 (New York, N.Y.: Praeger, 1981), 48–49.

64. See James Adams, *The Unnatural Alliance* (New York, N.Y.: Quartet, 1984) and Peter Bunce, "The Growth of South Africa's Defense Industry and its Israeli connection," *RUSI Journal,* no. 2 (June 1984).

65. Richard Bissell, *South Africa and the United States: The Erosion of an Influential Relationship* (New York, N.Y.: Praeger, 1982), 61.

66. Adams, *The Unnatural Alliance,* 109.

67. *Eight Days,* February 25, 1981.

68. *Aviation Week and Space Technology,* February 14, 1983, p. 17.

69. Robert E. Harkavy and Stephanie G. Neuman, "Israel" in James E. Katz, ed., *Arms Production in Developing Countries: An Analysis of Decision-Making* (Lexington, Mass.: D. C. Heath and Co., 1984), 212.

70. *Financial Times,* August 21, 1985.

71. Cornelius Castoriadis, *Devant la guerre* (Paris: Fayard, 1981).

72. *Armed Forces*, November 1983, p. 26.

73. *Defence Today*, no. 9, 89–90, 1985.

74. Norman L. Dodd, "ARMSCOR in 1985," *African Defence*, June 1985, p. 52.

75. John Reed, "ARMSCOR, Defence Talks to Commandant P. F. Marais," *African Defence*, January 1984, p. 24.

76. *Star*, September 19, 1981.

77. *Financial Mail*, September 11, 1981.

78. Adams, *The Unnatural Alliance*.

79. Pentagon Report, March 1986, cited in *South Africa Digest*, April 4, 1986.

80. See my *The United States and South Africa 1968–86: Constructive Engagement and Its Critics* (Durham, N. C.: Duke University Press, 1986), 206–207.

81. Ian Christie, *The Simonstown Agreement* (London: London Bureau, 1970), 10.

82. Ronald T. Pretty, "South African Valkeri multiple artillery rocket system," *Jane's Defence review* 4, no. 7 (1983), 649.

83. Cited in *Keesings Contemporary Archives*, May 29, 1981, p. 30888.

84. *Flight International*, January 19, 1985, p. 22.

85. R. K. Campbell, *Seapower and South Africa* (Pretoria: Institute for Strategic Studies Ad Hoc Publication No. 18, April 1984), 16.

86. J. E. Spence, "South Africa and the Defence of the West," *Survival* (March 13, 1971).

87. G. A. Malan, "The Strategic Importance of the RSA," *South Digest* (September 8, 1978), 5.

88. Zdenek Cervenka and Barbara Rogers, *The Nuclear Axis: Secret Collaboration between West Germany and South Africa* (London: Julian Friedman, 1978), 81.

89. *New York Times*, July 12, 1970.

90. Bissell, *South Africa and the United States*, 65.

91. *Scope Paper Memorandum from Chester A. Crocker to Secretary of State Alexander Haig*, May 14, 1981.

92. *Washington Post*, April 22, 1983.

93. Bernard Weimar, "United States and the Front Line States of Southern Africa: The Case for Closer Cooperation," *Atlantic Quarterly* 2, no. 1 (Spring 1984).

94. *Los Angeles Times*, April 24, 1984.

95. George Bush, "A New Partnership with Africa," extracts from an address to the Kenya Chamber of Commerce, Nairobi, November 19, 1982, *Southern Africa Record* (December 1982), 35.

96. *Wall Street Journal*, May 14, 1980.

97. Gerald J. Bender, "Angola: The Continuing Crisis and Misunderstanding," *International Affairs Bulletin* 7, no. 1 (1983), 4–13.

98. H. G. Wells, *Mr. Britling Sees It Through* (1916) cited in Barry Porter, *The Lion's share: a Short History of British Imperialism* (London: Longman, 1975), 235.

99. *Summary of World Broadcasts* (SWB) SU/7533/A51, January 6, 1984.

100. *New African*, August 1983.

101. Chester A. Crocker, "The Reagan Administration's Africa Policy: A Progress Report," address before the Fourth Annual Conference on International Affairs, U.S.-Africa Relations Since 1960, University of Kansas, November 10, 1983, *Department of State Bulletin*, 84:2082 (January 1984).

102. Gerald Bender, "The Reagan Administration and Southern Africa," *Atlantic Quarterly* 2, no. 3 (Autumn 1983), 238–239.

103. *Times* (London), September 24, 1985.

104. *International Herald Tribune*, September 3, 1985.

105. Winrich Kühn, "What Does the Case of Mozambique Tell Us About Soviet Ambivalence Toward Africa," *Africa Notes*, no. 46 (August 30, 1985).

106. Gillian Gunn, "Mozambique After Machel," *CSIS Africa Notes*, no. 67, December 29, 1986.

107. Gillian Gunn, unpublished ms., April 1987.

108. *Star International Weekly*, April 8, 1985.

109. *Africa Defence*, September 1985.

110. *Guardian*, October 21, 1986.

111. *Financial Times*, January 9, 1984.

112. Cited in *X-Ray*, May/June 1980.

113. Castoriadis, *Devant la guerre.*

114. *Guardian*, March 19, 1985.

115. *Rand Daily Mail*, March 31, 1983.

116. *Combatant*, no. 10 (1984).

117. *Financial Mail*, July 29, 1983.

118. *White Paper on Defence and Armaments Supply 1977* (Pretoria: Department of Defense, 1977), 4.

119. *White Paper on Defence and Armaments Supply 1986* (Pretoria: Department of Defense, 1986), 15. "The purpose of SADF is to create and maintain peaceful conditions in which government constitutional initiatives may develop fully."

120. *Cape Times*, January 1, 1985.

121. John Seiler and Deon Geldenhuys, "South Africa's Evolving State Security System," paper presented at the Study Group on the Armed Forces and Society of the International Political Science Association, West Berlin, September 1984, p. 14.

122. See Kenneth Grundy, *Soldiers Without Politics: Blacks in the South African Armed Forces* (Berkeley, Calif.: University of California Press, 1983), and C. J. Nothing, "Blacks, Coloureds and Indians in the South African Defence Force," *South Africa International* 11, no. 1 (July 1980): 21–28.

123. *South Africa: Time Running Out*, 247.

124. Grundy, "Bearing the burden of war," 217.

125. For the politics of "joint survival" see Heribert Adam, "Survival Politics: In Search of a New Ideology," in H. Adam and H. Giliomee, *The Rise and Crisis of Afrikaner Power* (Cape Town: David Philip, 1979), 128–144.

126. *Guardian*, March 17, 1985.

127. See, for example, the conclusions of the Geldenhuys Commission (1984–1986), whose main recommendation, after two years of deliberations, was that members of the Cape Coloured Corps be allowed to join other regiments or units at the discretion of the regiment or unit concerned.

128. *Newsweek*, September 29, 1980.

129. *San Francisco Examiner*, January 22, 1986.

130. Kenneth Adelman, *African Realities* (New York, N.Y.: Crane Russak and Co., 1980), 107.

131. Ronald Walters, "The Mystery Flash: Did South Africa Detonate a Nuclear Bomb?" Report by the Washington Office on Africa Education Fund, May 21, 1985.

132. Adams, *The Unnatural Alliance*, 18.

133. G. K. Keller, "Israeli-South African Trade: Analysis of Recent Developments," *Naval War College Review* (Spring 1980).

134. Leonard Spector, *The New Nuclear Nations* (Washington, D.C.: The Carnegie Endowment for Peace, 1985), 14.

135. *Le Monde*, September 17, 1985.

136. *Aerospace Daily*, May 1, 1985.

137. *Sunday Times* (London), March 13, 1977.

138. One of the problems facing South Africa is that ARMS-COR's official representation in the interdepartmental committees responsible for defining the threat the country may face in the future has inevitably added weight to the claim that the Republic has spawned a military-industrial complex every bit as competitive as its U.S. counterpart. As Joseph Schumpeter once wrote, it was "created by the wars that required it, [and] the machine now created the wars it required." Cited in J. Slater, "The Concept of a Military-Industrial Complex" in S. Rosen, ed., *Testing the Theory of the Military-Industrial Complex* (Lexington, Mass.: Lexington Books, 1973), 32.

139. Paul Johnson, *A History of the Modern World from 1917 to the 1980s* (London: Weidenfeld and Nicolson, 1983), 468–471.

140. *Observer* (London), March 18, 1984.

141. *Financial Times*, February 24, 1981.

Index

Numbers in *italics* denote figures; numbers followed by 't' denote tables.

shortages of, 33–34
USSR missile threat, 4
South African Defense Force
 (SADF)
 black soldiers, 83–84
 budget cuts, 80
 Citizen Force, 1, 29
 commitment to, viii
 conscription, 16
 counterinsurgency and, 7, 46
 declining numbers, 28
 desertions from, 16, 45
 evasion of service in, 17
 frontier defenses, 19–23
 growth of, 1–3, 28
 internal sabotage in, 45
 journal of, 27, 30
 NATO and, 68–69
 neutrality of, 82
 1985 offensive, 36
 permanent force, 1
 point defense system, 19
 roadblocks by, 12
 Special Defense Account, 78–79
 special forces, 47
 tank strength, 33
South African Navy (SAN)
 history of, 63–65
 search authority of, 69
 submarine program of, 66–67
South African Police (SAP)
 black uprisings and, 11
 limitations of, 11–12
 WHAM strategy, 14
South-West Africa People's
 Organization (SWAPO)
 costs of struggle, 45
 strength of, 42, 101n
 tribal opposition to, 87
 in Zambia, 30
South-West Africa Police, special
 forces, 46–47
South-West Africa Territory Force
 (SWATF), 86

Soviet Union (USSR)
 arms supplied by, 3, 27, 35, 61
 FLS and, 27
 Ovambo tribe and, 41
 SAN and, 65
 southern air umbrella, 35
 threat of, 70–71, 76
Soweto uprising, 3, 15
 black military and, 85
 deaths in, 10
 police and, 11
Special Defense Account, 78
Special forces, 46
Spence, Jack, 68
Stalin, Joseph, 11
State Security Council, CIA and,
 70
Stratocracy, 78
Submarine programs, 66–67
SWAPO. *See* South-West Africa
 People's Organization
SWAT. *See* South-West Africa
 Territory Force
Swaziland, border with, 19

Terrorism, 8, 40
Thunder Chariot Operation, 26,
 99n
Time factor, in security, ix
Townships
 development of, 9
 policing of, 10
 use of conscripts, 17
 See also specific townships
Transkei rebellion, 23
Tribalism, 87
Tutu, Bishop Desmond, 88
Tuutaleni, Jossy, 42

UDF. *See* United Democratic
 Front
UNITA. *See* National Union for
 the Total Independence of
 Angola